The Sky Turned Green
&
The Grass Turned Blue

Diane's Story

My Personal Journey as the Significant Other to an
M2F Transsexual

Diana Kelly

The Sky Turned Green
&
The Grass Turned Blue

Diane's Story

(My Personal Journey as the Significant Other to an
M2F Transsexual)

Publisher:
Green Sky Publishing, PO Box 2067, San Rafael, California 94912
Website/Contact:
https://greenskypublishing.com/dianakellyauthor/
Publishing platforms: IngramSpark

ISBN: 978-1-7326844-6-1
Library of Congress Control Number: 2018912312
1 2 3 4 5 6 7 8 9 10

Cover Design, Initial Visual Concept: Senet Kelly
Cover Design Technical Creation: Donald F. Kelly, II
Author Photos: Blink, Inc., Photographer, Subhrajit Bhatta
Editors: Suzanne Logan, Lily O'Brien and Ray Slater

This book is dedicated to all who seek their authentic self, and to all of those who love them.

Introduction

Until the time of this writing, very little has been written about what it means to be a significant other: wife, husband, partner, mother, father, sibling, child, cousin, or friend to a person who is a transsexual and who wants to make the difficult life transition from male to female, or female to male. My relationship with Jocelyn took place in the mid-to-late 1990s. Then, the term transgender was seldom heard in mainstream society in the United States, and even less was known about what it meant to be a transsexual.

Thankfully, in the past couple of years, there has been a spotlight shone on some of what it means to be a transgender or transsexual. Public figures such as Chaz Bono, had transitioned from female to male in 2009. Caitlyn Jenner transitioned from male to female in 2015. Also, in 2015, the movie *The Danish Girl*, starring Eddie Redmayne as artist Lili Elbe, who transitioned from male to female, and Alicia Vikander as Lili's significant other, Gerda Wegener, came to the big screen. The movie portrayed Lili's transition and Gerda's emotional struggle with Lili's transition. Each of these life stories has made the public more aware.

But I did not have these stories as reference. Nor could I find the kind of information I needed online, in libraries or in bookstores, that could help me understand what was at the core of Jack's desire. Jack wouldn't discuss it with me, and I knew my friends and family would not understand. There was no one I could talk to; I felt very alone. But regardless, I cared enough about Jack to try to open my mind to his reality. After much searching, I did find a book called *True Selves* by Mildred Brown and Chloe Ann Rounsley, which helped define transsexualism. But it was a book by Gilbert Herdt, called *Third Sex, Third Gender–Beyond Sexual Dimorphism in Culture and History*, that I found to be the most helpful. It showed me that there was more to transsexualism than a medical DSM code. In fact, it was not a modern phenomenon at all. In many cultures, gender nonconformity is considered nothing more than another way of life. What a relief! But where did that leave me? I still needed to understand how it would impact my relationship with Jack, and I had no answers for that. I knew I had decisions to make. Should I stay, or should I go? All I knew was that I loved Jack. That started me on a journey to understanding, which I had to navigate on my own.

Chapter 1

Prologue

I am an ordinary woman. Throughout the morning, the words had replayed in my mind like a broken record when the needle sticks. Attempting to bolster my self-confidence by using that phrase as an affirmation, I came to realize that all I had managed to do was to confirm my uncertainty. *I AM an ordinary woman*, I say aloud. *Or at least, I used to be.*

Like many women of the baby boomer era, I am fairly well educated, having gone to college. Living in the San Francisco Bay Area most of my life, I tended to be liberal in my politics and socially aware. Industrious, I began working at the age of fifteen. At the age of twenty-one, I married, and then, eighteen years later, found myself divorced. A mother of five growing children, four boys and a girl, my covey of kids was enough to set me apart from the majority of people I knew. But like many women in my situation, my life circled around work, home, and taking care of my children—an ordinary woman by most standards. That is, until I met Jack.

As you might have guessed, I fell in love again. But what happened with Jack—the details—this is where my story begins; until now, it's a story I have kept

1

mostly to myself. It's not a secret, but after all, who could possibly understand? There had been a pivotal moment—you know the kind—when you know that nothing will ever be the same again. And in *that* moment, I knew that *I* would never be the same again. The world as I knew it had turned upside down—the sky turned green and the grass turned blue.

I wondered if Tara would understand.

Tara had started two months before as the newest member of the executive administrative team at the company where I worked. Until now, our association had been through quick snippets of conversation during ten-minute coffee breaks. But today our managers are in meetings across town, giving us the rare afternoon off, so we are planning to meet for lunch. It would be a chance for us to get to know each other outside the office walls, and out of the earshot of others.

Tara seemed to have an open mind, and unlike some others, she didn't seem to jump to conclusions. My assessment was that I could talk to her. More than once, she had mentioned that she wanted to know what had happened between Jack and me. But knowing that the complexity of a ten-year relationship couldn't be explained in ten minutes, I had avoided getting into it. But today, I anticipated that she might have a list of questions.

As I scramble through my desk drawer, grabbing for my purse and the package that lay beneath, my inner voice called out that it was getting late.

I know that *Viva*, the popular North Beach restaurant, is only a few blocks away—I have plenty of time. I know my anxiety is raising its ugly head because the record player's needle skips again and my thoughts become stuck on what Tara will think.

You have to tell someone, sometime, I tell myself, as I descend the stairs to the building's lobby. *It's*

2

2006—times are changing. As I push open the heavy iron gate and step out onto Gold Street, I vow that if Tara asks, *sometime* will be today.

Chapter 2

Flower of the Mountain

The noon lunch crowd streams along Columbus Avenue under the August sun. I wade in, bypassing the meandering tourists stopping to admire the patina on the Coppola Building, before I fall into step with a group of elderly Chinese women chattering in Cantonese. Their pink plastic bags, each bursting with vegetables, swing in slow rhythm.

Come on People! Hurry up! Now, anxiety's voice fuels my irritation. As I glance about for a quick escape route, I happen to spot City Lights Bookstore across the street.

"Let's go in." I hear Jack's voice emerge from the past. "This is a great place!"

The voice tugs at me. I stop for a moment and look at my watch. There is no time. Trying to silence the memories, I pick up my pace as I walk through the throng of people along Columbus Avenue, but the effort to subdue my thoughts is to no avail. What happened on that long-ago Sunday afternoon continues to hover over and haunt me.

* * *

Even though I knew City Lights Bookstore for housing the works of many famous poets and prose

5

authors, including Jack Kerouac and Allen Ginsberg, and besides the fact that I had been an avid reader before the birth of my children, until that particular Sunday afternoon in the summer of 1990, I had never set foot in the store. On the other hand, Jack, who hailed from the East Coast and had traveled a lot, periodically rattled off titles of books he had purchased there over the years. "I used to come here anytime I made it to San Francisco," he had said.

Memory served how Jack had pushed the door open and led the way inside. Immediately, I had known why Jack was so drawn to the iconic North Beach bookstore. The perfume of paper and ink was present in the air. Wood floors creaked. Patrons whispered quietly among the stacks. An old man sat hunched on a bench with his face buried in a copy of *On the Road*. For a moment, I sensed what it felt like to be transported in time.

I had stopped at a section called Beat Poets when a book by the shop's owner, Lawrence Ferlinghetti, *The Secret Meaning of Things*, caught my eye.

Ironic, I think now. *Was the universe giving me a sign?*

I recall leafing through its pages while Jack marched purposefully ahead through the rows of books. *He must be looking for something in particular*, I had thought. I saw Jack reach for a volume and thumb his way through it.

"Find something interesting?" I asked, as I caught up and noticed the cover. James Joyce? "Yes! . . . yes." His countenance was reverent as he flipped through the book's pages. Then, pausing, he adjusted his glasses on his nose, cleared his throat, took a quick look at me, and began to read.

6

". . . after that long kiss I near lost my breath yes he said I was a flower of the mountain yes so we are flowers all a woman's body yes... that was why I liked him because I saw he understood or felt what a woman is"

Jack paused and looked at me with an expression that told me he was wearing his heart on his sleeve.

"That's beautiful, Jack," I said, but felt embarrassed when I noticed curious patrons were listening.

"Wait!" he said, as he held his index finger high before leaning in close to whisper.

". . . he kissed me under the Moorish wall . . . I asked him with my eyes to ask again yes and then he asked me would I yes to say yes my mountain flower yes I said yes I will Yes."

The words and Jack's warm breath on my cheek had caused me to shiver and blush. He finished the reading, allowing his voice to trail off in an expression of theatrical flourish.

Ulysses! Jack proclaimed, "I always loved that piece, Diane," he said, and he snapped the book shut.

Looking back, I remember thinking that Jack was such a romantic. A part of me wanted to believe that he was referring to his feelings for me. I remember how I had held onto the sentiment of the words for days and weeks and kept them close to my heart as my feelings for Jack grew. *Jack's the type of man I could spend my life with*, I had thought. In that moment, I had felt I was living in a perfect world.

7

Now I wonder how I will tell Tara that Jack was no ordinary man.

Chapter 3

Tara

I clutch at the package I carry, pressing it against my chest like a shield, as I teeter on the edge of the curb at Broadway and Columbus waiting for the light to change. My heartbeat quickens as I feel anxiety creep back in and flood my chest with a warm tingling sensation. I catch my breath.

"Just try to relax and breathe," the doctor had prescribed. His conclusion was that I had developed a form of post-traumatic stress disorder, commonly referred to as PTSD. "Not uncommon when your world goes upside down," he had said.

I wanted to relax. I wanted to be in the moment—I wanted to enjoy the day. I release my white-knuckled grip on the package I carry long enough to let my shoulders drop down and back, and I inhale slowly.

Just breathe! I think, as I concentrate on my exhale. *One—Two—Three—Four—Five! Now, inhale! One—Two—Three—Four—Five! Again*, the inner voice prompts. One more time, I exhale in slow rhythmic breaths.

I could not deny it *did* help. I begin to feel my anxiety ebb as I notice the crosswalk chirp its signal. A taxi whizzes by, nearly clipping an overly eager pedestrian about to step off the curb. It reminds me that being in the moment means staying alert.

Click, click, click. Tourists snap photos of "Big Al," Tommy gun in hand, as he eyes them from the sign high above street level. As I dodge the selfie-taking group, I notice a faded poster of Carol Doda sitting lopsided in a window of what once was the Condor Club, and remember how her sensational topless dance had drawn crowds to this street corner location in the 1960s, spurring the North Beach neighborhood of the beat poets to become a tourist go-to for Italian food, sensationalism, and sex. *What an unusual combination*, I thought, just as a barker called out from a doorway, "Come take a peek!" My glance in his direction, and down Broadway at the run-down strip clubs and porn studios, causes me to recall Jack's confession when I confronted him as to his whereabouts when he hadn't returned my late-night phone call. His eyes had darted furtively, and his cheeks had turned red, as he said he had gone to watch a sexy dancer-behind-glass.

I shake off the memory as I approach *Viva* and see a line that has formed outside. Tara texts that she has found a seat. Feeling grateful not to have to stand in line, I squeeze my way between the sardine-packed thirty-somethings standing just inside the door sipping wine and beer, as waiters bustle by with pitchers of water and the Three Tenors melodically sing *O Sole Mio* in the background.

As I survey the room that radiates the warmth and homey atmosphere of an Italian kitchen, the aroma of garlic and baked sourdough permeate the air. I feel a sense of relief when I see Tara wave from a corner table.

"You made it," says the fair-skinned young woman who stands to welcome me. A smile lights her hazelgreen eyes and her warm hug sets me at ease. She flips strands of long brown hair, streaked with tawny color, over her shoulders as we sit down.

"I'm so glad we have the opportunity to have lunch today," she states enthusiastically, paying no attention as the table wobbles and tips as I reach under it to grapple for a non-existent purse hook.

"Me, too," I say, placing my purse and package at my feet.

"I haven't been able to stop thinking about what you said about Jack!"

She had jumped right in sooner than I had anticipated. I smile, avoid eye contact, and seek to buy time by pausing to flip the menu over to look at the wine list before our waiter comes.

"How are you and Jake doing?" I ask, once the waiter takes our drink order.

"We are doing great!"

"Is there a long-range plan?"

"We haven't gotten to *that* discussion yet," she smiles, just as our Johnny-on-the-spot waiter sets two glasses of Chateau St. Jean merlot on our table.

"To an afternoon of girl-talk!" Tara says raising her glass.

"*Salute*," I gesture in return.

"Now," she says, even before taking a sip of the ruby liquid. "Tell me!" Her smile encourages, as she settles back into her chair.

"Where do I start?" I ask aloud. I sense my anxiety beginning to return. I try to cover by taking a bite of warm bread and take a moment to wash it down with wine, and then carefully take time to wipe my fingers on the red-and-white-checkered napkin that lays on my lap.

"You started to tell me about seeing him at the top of the stairs," Tara suggests. Then, as quickly as she

11

asks the question, she backs away from it, adding, "I'm sorry." Her brow furrows. "I've had rough times in some of my own relationships. Some I don't ever want to talk about, let alone ever remember again! I shouldn't assume you are comfortable talking about it."

I knew she didn't want to let it go.

"But I *am* curious," she adds.

"As relationships go, ours wasn't all that different," I lie.

"You never did say how you met him," she prods.

"I *would* like to tell you about it," I say, remembering the vow I had made to myself. "But it's a long story, Tara." I reach under the table to retrieve the package and hand it to her.

Tara looks surprised, but reaches into the thick manila envelope and eagerly retrieves its contents.

"You've written about it?" Her eyes grew wide as she glances at the first pages.

I nod. "I started. I am trying to. It was such a difficult time. I had no one to talk to, no way to express my feelings about what went on. The only thing I could think of to do was to write about it, try to get it outside of myself, and try to find perspective and balance again. I have even thought, maybe someday, I can help others who might have a similar experience."

As Tara continues to browse through the typed pages, I find words come easily with the help of the Chateau St. Jean. I seize the moment and begin to explain.

Chapter 4

The Singing Diva

"I'll never forget the first time I saw him," I begin. "It was the week after New Year's, in 1990. I can't forget the date, because we had just had that big earthquake, the Loma Prieta, a couple of months before."

"In Watsonville, near Santa Cruz . . . my hometown," Tara replies. It was a date Tara wasn't about to forget either.

"Yes," I say. "He passed by my office door taking long, quick strides—a dark-suited flash in my peripheral vision. I had no idea who he was. A bit later, he reappeared with the CEO who was taking him on a facility tour."

Tara's attention is shifting back and forth between the written pages she holds and my verbal comments, with an occasional uh-huh, and sometimes a quizzical look. As she concentrates on reading, I stop talking, and allow my mind to travel down memory lane.

* * *

"This is Dr. Jack Martin." Mr. French, the CEO, introduced the newest member of the hospital's physician staff to the medical records office group. "We are very fortunate to have him join us," he said, before elaborating on the doctor's smart-as-a-whip credentials.

He's Harvard smart, I thought, as I remembered reading his bio in the hospital newsletter while eating lunch in the employee lunchroom.

As the rest of the steno pool gawked, I made my own evaluation of Dr. Martin, as he stood in what seemed like brooding silence, with his arms crossed in self-hugging fashion, shifting his weight from one foot to the other. *He has sad eyes*, I thought, and for a brief moment, wondered why.

Tall and thin—he does have a silver spoon air about him—it fits, I said to myself, thinking again about his East Coast background. What didn't fit was that Dr. Martin seemed uncomfortable in the spotlight. Most of the docs would have enjoyed this kind of attention.

"Check out his tie!" I heard a co-worker whisper to the woman seated next to her.

I, myself, had noticed his black suit and contrasting rose-colored shirt. I had thought, *sharp dresser!* The black tie was an eye-catcher, imprinted with the bold caricature of a woman in the stance of a singing diva. Could it be Jessica from *Who Framed Roger Rabbit?* It sure looked like her, with the same formfitting, rose-red evening gown and the same long red hair, tossed back. Her arms were swathed in black elbow-length evening gloves and opened wide towards the steno pool audience in true diva fashion, as if singing, "I'm here! Admire me!"

It's certainly not the usual doctor tie. I smiled and silently congratulated him on daring to be different. *He has a sense of humor*, I thought, *or perhaps he is just eccentric*. Having made the judgment, I dismissed the dark leather bag slung haphazardly over his shoulder, reminiscent of a woman's purse.

* * *

I swirl the last of the red wine in my nearly empty glass and remember how Jack's ties soon became his trademark and part of the ongoing hospital staff gossip.

"You said you worked for Jack?" Tara's question brings me out of my daydream.

"Only now and then," I answer. "At that point in time, I was always looking for ways to bring in a few extra dollars, and word got out that the new doc was looking for someone to help him set up his office."

"So, that's how you got to know him?"

"Yes," I nod. "I'd go in on a Saturday to do some filing when he was there catching up on his charts. We would talk."

I pause, thinking a moment before going on about all of the things that had made Jack special.

"I enjoyed our conversations. He had a quick mind and a zany sense of humor. He possessed a spirit of adventure, often speaking of his desire to travel. He loved music and art. When I met him, I was taking night classes in art at City College. Did I ever mention that?"

Tara shook her head. "You never told me you went to college while you were raising your kids? How did you manage that? Night classes?"

"Yes. I had always wanted a college education and it had been difficult to pursue when the kids were small. But as they got older, I had managed to find time. Jack applauded my effort and was supportive. We had long discussions about art history, and, of course, by virtue of our jobs, medicine—for hours. He was like a walking encyclopedia. He would say he was good at remembering trivia, but it was more than that. Once he let it slip that he had a photographic memory. The fact was, he was intellectually impressive, a good doctor,

15

and excellent at diagnosing the ailments of his patients. I respected him for that."

"It sounds like a mutual admiration society. I'm sure he was also very impressed by what *you* were managing to do," Tara says, shining a light back on me. "So, when did it become personal?"

"We were both divorced. He said he had never had children; he and his wife had preferred to travel. Initially, I didn't think of dating."

"I can see why you would have enjoyed spending time with him," Tara interjects. "There you were, a divorced woman with five kids, struggling to make ends meet. How old were you when you met him?"

"Forty-five."

"And he was?" Tara asks.

"Forty-three."

"There you go! You had an opportunity to enjoy adult conversation and companionship with someone your own age, with a similar background. Who wouldn't understand that?"

I nod, relieved that she did.

"We became friends," I admit. "But, dating? I didn't think of dating, I didn't have a romantic interest. He wasn't my type—not like the men I was usually attracted to—or that were attracted to me."

"Was he handsome?" Tara asks expectantly, with a glint in her eye.

"An average guy. Nice-looking, mature, thinning hair." I say. "Average-looking, but he took care of himself."

"What was the main attraction, then?"

"The more I got to know him, Tara, the more I realized he had characteristics that I really liked. And, then he surprised me by asking me out. Until then, it hadn't occurred to me he might actually be interested in *me* that way."

I sit back, realizing the lunch crowd is beginning to dissipate. Checking my watch, I see we've been talking almost an hour. Tara notices too.

"I think we need another glass of wine," Tara laughs, as she signals the waiter. "Shall we eat? I'm hungry for pasta."

"I'm game," I say. The wine *had* relaxed me. Or, maybe I was just comfortable with Tara. Either way, I was feeling grateful. I had found someone I could talk to. Today would be my own coming out.

"I hope I'm not boring you," I say to Tara.

"Are you kidding?" she answers. "Please go on. I have all afternoon and we haven't had lunch yet," she says with a smile, as she reaches for a menu.

"I liked Jack a lot, Tara," I say. *But some did not*, I thought, and as Tara checked over the menu, I remembered an evening I was called in to work, and what Mark had said.

Chapter 5

Bitter Pill

I felt the weight of the heavy door of the underground garage as I pushed it open and exited into a stairwell that led up to a pitch-dark parking lot. The metal door slammed shut behind me with a resounding thud, and the well-lit interior of the garage disappeared behind me. My eyes fought to adjust to the darkness.

"I'll come right away!" I had responded when the phone call came, though I felt a sharp pang of motherly guilt at leaving my children home alone on a Friday evening, and this one in particular, since Jack had asked if I would go to dinner Saturday night.

Two evenings away from the kids . . . maybe I can get back home within an hour, I had thought. As Alex began to whine, I handed sixteen-year-old David the pot of spaghetti.

"Mommmie!" Kristie wailed. My youngest looked as if she might cry. "You promised to read me a story!" she pouted, stomping her foot for emphasis.

"I know, Kristie. I'm sorry, honey. Work needs me." I said. "But I'll be back as quick as I can."

"It's okay, Mom. Go!" David said, urging me toward the door. "Don't worry! I've got this."

I smiled proudly at how he had stepped up, but felt a twinge of sadness as I realized David was no longer a kid. Adding to his responsibilities, he was always willing to babysit his younger siblings on nights like this. He understood the extra money that I made on call helped all of us. I appreciated his help and tried to make sure he knew it. He had grown up too fast. The divorce six years before had fractured our family. I had given my all for sixteen years. "For better or worse," the vows had said, but no one said how worse it could become. Still, I was not devoid of feelings of guilt, even though the five children were better off, and I was grateful for David.

"I will be back in time for popcorn, and Kristie, I will read you a story before bedtime," I said, in an attempt to reassure the sad-faced group. I whispered, "Thank you!" to David, as I picked up my purse and car keys.

Having given each of the small children a kiss and a hug before their tears fell, I slipped out the door. I knew David would find a quick way to provide a distraction. I watched him hand Kristie her Barbie and saw him slip a cartridge into the Nintendo and hand Alex the controller.

Lost in thought about home, I nearly missed the three figures hidden in the shadows of the dark parking lot. I saw their faces and tattoos illuminated as one of them lit a cigarette, just as I noticed the trio had begun to move in my direction. Startled, I pulled my purse close and calculated the distance up the ramp to the hospital's emergency department.

Run! The thought raced through my mind just as a Yellow Cab turned into the emergency parking lot. The bright light of its high beams caused the three to shrink back into the shadows. I took advantage and darted up the emergency room entrance ramp.

A close call! I breathed a sigh of relief when I saw the emergency room's security guard through the sliding glass door.

Friday nights on a full moon bring out the crazies. It was a mantra often repeated by ER personnel.

I shivered at the thought and recalled the nursing supervisor's statement when she called earlier. "You're needed to prepare a report for a patient transfer to UCSF—a young Latino gunshot victim."

Maybe there was something to this full moon mantra, I thought.

The heavy metal-framed glass doors at the top of the ER ramp slid open. I prepared myself for the blast of warm air, along with the familiar stringent odor of antiseptic and other pharmaceuticals that never failed to assault my senses. The regular Friday night throng of sick children and the elderly crowded the waiting room, along with some others that appeared just to be down and out. Staff nurses bustled along the hallway, and a gurney rolled in my direction. I hurried across the hall towards the open elevator doors.

"Diane!" I heard Trina, the ER transcriptionist call out from the reception desk.

I waved, not wanting to be rude, but not wanting to slow down either. I beat the closing elevator door and slid inside. The closed doors silenced the hum of voices, the unhappy cries of ailing children, and the rant of a schizophrenic. It lent a moment of peace.

I pushed the down button, but was caught off-balance. Gripping the handrail, I realized that the floor indicator said that I was going up.

I thumb-punched the down button frantically in a fruitless attempt. The elevator door opened on the surgical floor and a hand reached in to hold the door open. In automatic response, I stepped back further into the elevator, as I anticipated a gurney rolling in. Instead, I heard his voice.

"Goodnight, Nancy! See you in the morning," he said with a wave of his hand. As he backed into the elevator, he slowly released his hold on the door, still unaware of my presence.

Silently, I watched his blue scrubs pulled taut across the broad shoulders of his muscular frame as he pulled on his worn leather jacket. He pulled off his blue surgical cap, stuffed it into his jacket pocket and stepped back. He leaned against the wall opposite me. Tiredness made the lines of his handsome face even more pronounced. He sighed under the strain of what I sensed was hours in the surgical suite. He needed sleep, and to get off his feet.

I wished it were anyone else but him.

"Hi, Mark!" I said cheerfully, before he looked up. His eyes registered surprise, and then sparked in recognition. The sexual tension, so familiar in our past, electrified the space between us. The moment became awkward. His eyes shifted nervously as he examined the lit numbers. As the car began its descent, I held tight to the elevator's handrail.

"How are you?" he finally asked in his deep, throaty voice, barely risking a glance towards me. His musky scent mixed with Armani permeated the air, igniting memories of our closeness three years before.

"Okay!" I answered, trying to focus, mustering up an air of conviction and a smile. "You?" I countered.

"I've been busy." He sighed, running his hand through his curly, blonde hair. "It's that full moon, you know," he said with a wry smile. When he chanced another glance, his intense, dark blue eyes captured mine.

"Kind of late for you, isn't it, and on a Friday night?" His smile teased now. His gravelly voice deepened, and his eyes began to dance with mischief, as they gave me his trademark once-over.

"Yes," I nodded, recognizing the need to keep the conversation about work. A flush of heat rushed to my face at his look, but I reminded myself that he and I were through.

"An emergency call," I babbled. "They needed the report done tonight—a patient transferring to UCSF. As you know, I can always use the overtime."

I had Mark's attention. "The gunshot? We just finished patching him up. We stopped the bleeding, but the kid needs the specialists at UCSF if he has any chance at making it." A look of concern etched his face. Mark cared.

"He's only seventeen! When will these kids learn?" he said with a hint of anger. He had sons, too.

I started to inch towards the front of the elevator. Anticipating my escape, he made his move.

"Wait!" Mark said, stepping to block my way as the door opened. He fixed his eyes intently on mine.

"What?" I asked, uncertain if I wanted to hear his answer. But his question wasn't at all what I expected.

"What are you doing, Diane?" Mark's voice was low, but agitated; I knew immediately he wasn't asking about work. "What are you doing with that guy?"

Thrown off guard, I looked into the hallway beyond the elevator's partially open door and hoped someone was waiting to board. The hallway was deserted.

I was trapped and did not want to have this conversation.

"I mean it, Diane," he continued. "What are you doing with that guy?"

"By that guy, do you mean, Jack?" I knew exactly who Mark meant, but two could play this game and I needed time to think about what I might say next. "You wouldn't understand."

"Wait just a minute, Diane. Please, hear me out." His voice was pleading. He placed his hand on my arm as I tried to move past.

"No, Mark!" I said angrily as I shook free. "This is different. He's different. It's not what you think!"

What *did* Mark think? Could he understand that Jack and I had found many interests in common? Jack's challenging intellect and adventurous spirit provided endless possibilities for companionship. It was none of Mark's business that Jack and I had become friends. But in my own defense, I continued.

"Maybe there's a chance for a real . . ."

"A real what?" Mark stopped me in mid-sentence with a look of disbelief. "Do you seriously believe you can have a lasting *relationship* with this guy? What— you think he might marry you some day? Come on! A woman with five kids. Think about it!"

As he moved in closer, I felt his body heat.

"Like I told you once before," he continued, lowering his voice, his breath touching my hair. "Some women aren't meant for that kind of relationship. You need to have fun. Forget about that other stuff! I know you! He isn't the right one for you. Believe me he's not."

"Like you?" I interjected, stepping back. The sadness I felt at hearing his words quickly turned to anger.

Stolen moments of our clandestine affair crossed my mind in lightening-like fashion, as I remembered our passion. Mark had been right in one regard; Jack did not seem testosterone-driven like Mark and countless other men I had known in the past. Jack had never even attempted to kiss me. Men I had known since my divorce seemed only interested in one thing, and that did not involve an interest in companionship, or developing a relationship. Jack *was* different. Our

24

relationship wasn't driven by sex. We were friends. Jack had expressed a desire for companionship right from the start.

"I need a tour guide. I have a list of places I'd like to see," Jack had said. "I like spending time with you! Would you be willing to take some time to show me around the city?" Knowing that Jack could have asked any one of countless women to accompany him, but he had asked me, had renewed my faith in possibility. And more, I felt respected.

What I knew of Jack and our plan to meet the next evening for dinner to talk about the office, helped strengthen my conviction. Mark was right. Jack was not a wham-bam-thank-you ma'am kind-of guy. He was not like Mark at all.

"I remember what you told me, Mark!" My anger spoke. "That's why we don't see each other anymore! Maybe being with this person and that person—no commitment, no expectation—is the life you want to live, but that's not for me! I want more for myself, and more for my kids!"

What Mark didn't know was that I wanted male friends. I didn't have a marriage expectation at this point in time. I didn't want to move in with someone, or have them move in with me. I was raising my kids, and I planned to do it my own way. I didn't need, or even want that kind of help. I did hope for an exclusive, committed relationship with a man. Eventually, I hoped to build a relationship with someone that would last until that point in time when my mom duties were not my major focus, and when I could consider a life of my own.

Mark stepped back. My words had hit home. He changed his tactic and now implored.

"Diane, I've seen him with people here at work. He isn't who you think he is. I don't know what it is. There is just something that doesn't feel right about him. Something tells me he is not the one for you!"

Mark's frustration was evident by the strained tone of his voice. Though put off by his insistence, I sensed he was partially correct. A nurse had approached me, quizzing me about Jack. I understood then that not everyone liked him. *Not everyone would warm up to him*, I had thought. Jack was hired to make changes in an established institution. I realized that and dismissed what I took as snide comments.

The elevator door buzzed at being held open too long and I ducked under Mark's outstretched arm, escaping into the hallway. I walked quickly toward my office, as Mark continued to hold the elevator door open and watch my retreat.

"Don't worry about me, Mark!" I called, as I looked over my shoulder and turned the key in the office door lock. "I think I know Jack a lot better than you think I do."

Yet, as the office door closed behind me, I felt as if I had swallowed a bitter pill.

Chapter 6

The Kiss

Fog fingers crept over the crest onto Turk Street as we turned right onto Baker. They billowed, stretched and cascaded towards us, pushed by a breeze blowing from the west. I recalled that after searching the dark street for a place to park, Jack had pulled over and maneuvered his tiny new car between a battered Ford pickup truck and a rusted-out light-blue Plymouth.

Mark's words of the night before had bothered me, but while I wasn't in a frame of mind to want to second-guess him, I was still trying to put his words into perspective. *Perhaps Mark is jealous?* I decided. *That's probably it.*

The Jack I knew was fun, energetic, and full of surprises. The past week had been no exception. I smiled as I thought of how Jack had stopped by my office earlier in the week, sporting a sheepish grin and asked, "Big or small? Red or black? Convertible or hard-top?"

Without thinking, I had replied, "Red convertible," before he had a chance to show me the glossy car brochures he took from his shoulder bag.

Two days later, he had led me out to the hospital's physician lot to show me the tiny red sports car. My surprise was not that Jack had purchased the car, but that he purchased *my choice*. His surprise had pulled me in. I had begun to feel that Jack cared about me.

The night had been a perfect evening. Jack was eager to try a new restaurant and had driven to the North India restaurant, near Union Street. As we enjoyed the Tandoori chicken, we laughed about the chilly but exhilarating top-down ride in the new car through the city streets, and then switched gears to commiserate over the ups-and-downs of the workweek. As I sipped the last of my mango lassi, Jack began to grin from ear-to-ear.

"I have a surprise for you!" he had blurted out. "I want to show you my apartment."

I remembered how I bubbled with enthusiasm as we left the restaurant and thought, *Mark's wrong! I want to know more about Jack, and seeing where he lives will give me more insight into the person he is.*

* * *

"He asked you out?" Tara asks, as she finishes glancing over the menu.

"Yes," I smiled. "Dinner."

"Had you ever seen where he lived?"

"Funny you should ask," I replied, feeling like she had read my mind. "No. Jack mentioned he would show me his apartment when he had a proper chair for me to sit on. He had been waiting for his belongings to come from out-of-state."

"Weren't you curious?"

"Of course I was."

"So how long had you known him at this point?" Tara quizzes.

"About three months. We had been spending more and more time together, mostly going out for dinner, and just talking."

As Tara picks up the manuscript and again, flips over a page, and continues to read, I remember that as Jack and I left the restaurant that particular night and walked along Webster Street towards the Cow Hollow garage, he took my hand. He held it tight. In an unexpected flutter of feelings, I realized that maybe I was beginning to care.

* * *

"We're here!" he said excitedly. "It's up there, on the third floor. You're going to love the view!"

Jack scrambled out of the car, quickly stepping around it to open my door, extending his hand, gently tugging on mine. I felt like a princess. He steadied me as I stepped out onto the sidewalk. I was grateful that he parked close, as the damp night air blew, straightening my hair, and curling my skirt around my bare legs. *He's a gentleman*, I thought, and added yet another point to the list I had created.

I peered through the swirling gray mist towards a cramped narrow entrance behind a small concrete stoop guarded by a heavy metal gate. Coming up the hill, we had skirted bunkers of low-cost housing. I knew Jack had taken his time to search for an apartment with a view. "It's San Francisco! Who wouldn't want a view?" he had asked. That said, and aware of Jack's income level, I had set an expectation, and this didn't rise to it.

I craned my neck, looking up through the foggy darkness. I wondered which one was Jack's apartment when I saw a trail of beige whip in the wind in a ghostly pattern. *A curtain? Who doesn't close their window?*

"I couldn't have gotten closer if I tried!" he said proudly. He had reclaimed my attention. "It certainly helps having a small car in the big city." He looked at me, smiled broadly, and said "Good choice!"

Jack's animated excitement overrode my apprehension.

Bracing back the silver-toned gate, Jack unlatched the steel-framed glass door, catching it before it could bang as it swung inward from the push of the strengthening wind. Quickly stepping inside the foyer, my high-heels clicked loudly on the pink-veined marble tile of the floor. A large mirror hung over a narrow, rough-hewn metal table. On it, a vase, speckled with silver, held a huge dust-covered bouquet of multi-colored plastic chrysanthemums. Garish light from a gaudy chandelier made of reflective glass and tiny bulbs illuminated a sign taped to the door of the elevator that read, "Out of Service."

Without hesitation, Jack strode towards the concrete slab stairs.

"Come on! It's only three flights up!" he chided, suggesting a race as he took two steps at a time.

Holding on to the banister, I gingerly made my way up the stairs, as his hurried steps caused the stairs to shake.

"Come on!" He encouraged again, before jumping down and back a step or two. He knew very well that he was causing more sway. His laugh echoed off the hard surface of the foyer below, as he peered down at me from the landing above.

Reaching the third-floor level, I leaned against the corridor wall and adjusted my sea legs as Jack fumbled through his pockets for the door key. Watching him, I felt I had found not only a friend, but also, a playmate.

"Damn! They were supposed to fix the lock!" Jack cursed with impatience, a side of him I had not seen before.

The latch released and the door swung inward. Jack's face relaxed with relief. A flourishing sweep of his outstretched arm and a slight bow invited me to cross the threshold into a tiny, carpeted entry.

* * *

"So, what did you think of his place," Tara asks, putting aside a page to take a small sip of wine.

"I could almost see the whole apartment as I stood in the entry," I say. "There was a small bathroom to the left, and a narrow shoebox kitchen, complete with espresso maker to the right. Bright- colored towels with abstract designs hung near the sink, and perfectly coordinated potholders hung next to the stove. A small dining nook was stacked with unopened Mayflower moving boxes. Directly ahead of me was an old wall furnace, and next to that, a closed door to a room beyond."

My mind's eye saw Jack as he moved quickly to block my way. "Don't go in there!" he said, pulling on the door's knob, making sure it was closed securely. "This is my junk room." I imagined the small bedroom crammed with more unpacked moving boxes, and miscellaneous furniture pieces. I did not know that the beige curtain I had seen trailed from an open window.

"Jack took my hand and asked me to close my eyes before he led me through a large, sparsely furnished living room. Then he said, 'Open your eyes.' We had stopped at a floor-to-ceiling wall of glass. I stood, transfixed. The panorama that lay out before me was beautiful. I stood spellbound; I could hardly speak!"

"Jack asked me to sit on the futon sofa near the window. Entranced, I could not sit down. I felt I was on the edge of a precipice. Below, the fog had settled thick on the hillside like a soft gray blanket. Above it, against the night sky, San Francisco's city lights sparkled like jewels. In the distance, a beacon flashed on Alcatraz, and further west trailed the arching span of orange and yellow lights that was the Golden Gate Bridge. Taillights flowed east on Market Street towards the Bay Bridge.

It was then I understood why Jack had chosen that location. The night view was beautiful."

"I can imagine what it might have been like, from my own experience atop Twin Peaks—absolutely stunning," says Tara.

"Breathtaking," I affirmed.

I was not ready to divulge to Tara what happened next.

As I had turned to exclaim my wonder at the view, I had felt Jack's hand touch my back and his arm encircle my waist. He turned me slowly and leaned his body against mine. I sensed his next move as his face brushed against my hair. Speaking unintelligible words softly in my ear, his breath was warm against my cheek. I closed my eyes in anticipation as his lips pressed against mine ever so gently, too gently . . . soft, too soft . . . tepid . . . impotent.

I stepped back, feeling confused. I worked to regain my composure as I watched passion melt Jack's face into an unusual softness, and wistful submission. A weak sigh escaped his lips. His eyes penetrated mine, asking questions for which I had no answers.

Chapter 7

Someone to Love

I paused in my narrative, long enough to drain the last drops of wine from my glass, and to mull over the inexplicable feeling of ambivalence that had accompanied Jack's kiss. Undaunted by my momentary silence, Tara seized the opportunity to engage two young men seated at a nearby table, asking for their wine recommendation, before motioning the waiter to bring us a bottle of Far Niente cabernet.

"Let's splurge!" she says, without a second thought.

I laugh as the waiter uncorks the bottle.

"Are we sure this is a good idea? I feel I may be passing my limit!"

"We have all afternoon," Tara says laughing, dismissing my concern.

Clearly, she is up for whatever would come next, and is in no hurry to end our conversation. I had relaxed. I felt better than I had in a long while. Further affirmation of how much I had needed to talk.

The waiter pours the deep red liquid into our glasses and takes our pasta order as the Three Tenors sing *Maria*. We raise our wine glasses, and catch the eyes of the two young men seated nearby as they raise theirs.

"*Salute!*" We say in unison, and then watch as they put their focus back on each other.

"So, did you feel that you learned more about Jack by seeing where he lived?" Tara asks, getting back into my story.

I think for a moment before answering. *How much do I want to divulge?* I am still not sure.

"Yes," I say, still thinking about the kiss. "Did I mention that it wasn't physical attraction that drew me to Jack? He wasn't my usual type. He held a different interest for me—companionship and conversation. It felt good to have a friend. Thinking about it now, I believe I regarded Jack as my muse."

And I was his, I think, and there is a momentary realization of the irony of it. An irony I am not sure I am ready to share.

"Your muse? How so?" Tara asks.

"I viewed my interaction with Jack as inspiration to work toward a better life for myself and for my children. I wasn't poor, but my funds were limited. My kids came first, and that didn't leave much left over for frills. I didn't have much of a social life. Jack's lifestyle of success and the unencumbered freedom he seemed to have was very different from my own. In some ways, spending time with him allowed me to live the dream.

"He also loved good food," I say, taking a moment to poke my fork into the steaming Pasta Pescatore the waiter had placed in front of me.

"He worked hard and played hard, and most of the time he did what he wanted to do. My life . . . well, there was no comparison. The way Jack lived was a fascination—carefree, spontaneous and curious. Men I had known liked to sit around and watch football and baseball. Jack wasn't like that. He wanted to go, and to explore, and he liked having me along."

"I can see why you would enjoy time with him," Tara acknowledges.

"Can you? He was a lot of fun to be with," I say.

How could I possibly explain all that Jack meant to me? Before Jack, I had been out of touch with the life that was going on around me. Colors seemed more vibrant when he was around. I had not even been to a Starbucks until Jack took me, and the idea of sitting around, relaxing in coffee shops, was something I had never thought about. It was a simple pleasure that so many people took for granted, and it was totally foreign to me.

"Listen!" I say, as I stop my thought in mid-sentence. "That's Pavarotti singing. Jack introduced me to opera—to Verdi—to jazz! In a nutshell, Jack expanded my view of life!"

"What did the kids think?" Tara probes.

I smile. "They liked him. In the beginning of our relationship, he would often want to include them in outings. He suggested trips to Golden Gate Park, the zoo, took them to movies, and insisted on taking all of us to see Cirque du Soleil! You've been?"

"Art and music in motion," she affirms. "It must have been a real treat for them."

"It was. More, Jack would take time with the boys to explain science-related things—like astronomy," I say. "I remember one afternoon when we took the kids to the planetarium. Later that same evening, Jack came back by the house and surprised them with a telescope so they could view the rings of Saturn and examine at the moon up close. Jack seemed to enjoy the children's excitement. Brian, in particular, loved science. Jack always seemed to enjoy sharing his knowledge and was patient to explain."

Tara shakes her head, acknowledging his action. "Was he into sports and cars—most men seem to be?"

"Sports, no, but he liked nice cars, especially sporty ones. He took time with Kristie, too. She's such a girly-girl. One afternoon, at her insistence, he sat patiently and allowed an eight-year-old to paint his fingernails with pink polish. Then, he continued to play her game, insisting on wearing the manicure home. She was thrilled."

"So, the evening you went to his apartment . . ."

Bless Tara, I think. *She knows how to keep a conversation on track.*

"You mentioned you didn't think you were his type. But something must have changed. What happened?"

She wants to get to the meat of it, I think, remembering another evening. *I might as well jump in feet first!*

"Jack, as it turned out, was an incurable romantic," I say, not really sure yet how to address what happened. "Another evening, he asked me over. It had turned cold and wet. When I arrived, candles lit the living room. The large windows overlooking the city were spotted with rain and sparkled with reflected color from the city lights below. If that wasn't enough to set a mood, two cups of steaming hot chocolate sat on a small table, and a lime-green comforter on the opened futon lay tossed back, inviting."

"Isn't that a good thing? Sounds cozy," Tara chuckles, and her eyes twinkle. "It sounds like your relationship didn't stay platonic?"

"It didn't," I say, thinking about the turn in our relationship, the feelings that came over me, and the things I had not understood. "He was so different from the men I had dated. I was never sure what to expect. He was unpredictable. Sometimes I found his behavior confusing. I was not sure what to think."

"How so?" Tara says, looking puzzled, sensing my reservation as I hesitate, wondering if I should go on.

36

"You are referring to 's-e-x'?" she asks, not waiting for confirmation. "You're a woman, he's a man. How is that confusing?"

"Let me go back," I say, deciding to try to explain what was then unexplainable. "When he kissed me the first time, it wasn't what I expected. Truth is, I did not know how to react. There was something about how it made me feel something I could not put my finger on. I attributed it to inexperience, or maybe to shyness, but then I thought, *this isn't his first rodeo!* He had been married for a number of years. Do you know what I mean? Yet, I guess I felt . . . I felt I would need to be the teacher."

"Ohh!" Tara says, thinking she knows what I am about to say. "Because you're the older woman," she smiles. "Or was he was inhibited—missionary position only."

"Actually, Tara, neither. And he certainly wasn't inhibited—not at all. But he *was* mainly interested in oral sex."

"A blow job, that's all he wanted?" Tara bristles.

"No, Tara! For him it was about giving, not receiving," I say, feeling a blush of heat and unsure if I want to continue. "I was not prepared for that. It was not my experience to have a man want to be as pleasure-giving as Jack was. I felt awkward and uncomfortable and felt that maybe it was *I* who needed the teacher!"

Taking a breath, I wait a moment to let my words sink in and wash down a bite of pasta with the flavorful cabernet.

"So, you were surprised that you were not able to predict him—not your average guy, or the kind of guy you were used to," she says, trying to sort it out. "You *did* have *regular* sex, though, didn't you?"

"Yes, but not ordinarily. What you and I might call regular sex didn't seem to be Jack's interest."

There! I said it. I feel like I have been to confession.

"Initially, I didn't know what to make of it," I say, acknowledging that she was right. "Over time, I realized it was the way he was. But there was a lingering thought as to why it seemed to be his preference."

"Did you ever talk about it?" she asks quietly, noting my discomfort.

"Only in a roundabout way," I answer. "I didn't want to offend him. You know how men are. I feared my questions would bring about an unwelcome response. I made the choice to ignore my feelings because I did not want to lose him or his friendship."

I pause to swirl my wine around the glass. *My mistake*, I thought. *Would Jack have confided in me sooner that he didn't feel comfortable with himself, if I hadn't been so afraid to ask questions in the beginning of our relationship, when things didn't feel quite right?*

"Tara, I know that when I met Jack, I wanted a relationship that wasn't just about sex. I wanted a different type of connection with a man. I wanted friendship and companionship, too. Sex has its place, don't get me wrong, but I wanted the total package. I thought that with Jack there might be that chance." I sigh. "It seems ironic now. I was so blind."

"Ironic? Blind?" Tara begins, just as the two men sitting at the nearby table get up to leave hand-in-hand and motion a goodbye. Tara follows my glance and simultaneously we wave goodbye.

"You know, Diane, relationships between people, they're all different." Tara's eyes follow the two before she adds, "By the way, did I ever mention that my sister is gay?"

38

"No. You didn't," I say, surprised, and welcome for the shift in subject.

"It was hard on our parents at first," she says matter-of-factly. "Most of us hope for a relationship, or as you called it, a connection. For some, it's friendship, for some, love. My sister and her partner found love. It was a surprise—no, a shock to us when she came out, but gradually acceptance came. Now, together, they have a loving family, kids and all. Truth be told, we should all be so lucky."

"I can't agree with you more, Tara!" I say, realizing that Tara might understand more than I could have ever realized.

"As I see it, Diane," Tara continues, "You were hoping for what any of us might want—someone to love!"

Chapter 8

The Marlboro Man

I am grateful that Tara understands. She is right. Almost everyone hopes to find someone to love, who will love them in return. Isn't wanting someone to love inherent in our nature?

Excusing herself at the melodic ring of her cell phone, Tara steps outside to take the call and leaves me to pick at the remaining few crumbs of sourdough bread. I glance toward the empty table where the two young men had sat and thought about another couple I had watched walk arm-in-arm several years before—on a January afternoon in 1996.

* * *

"It's one of those days it feels good to be alive," I had exclaimed to Jack in spontaneous, grateful acknowledgement of living in the moment.

I inhaled crisp, clean air as we left the parking garage and walked towards the North Tower of the medical center's entrance. As I listened to Jack recount the events of his day, I took note of a tall man as he approached an iron rail that bordered a nearby veranda. Weak and frail, he leaned his bony arms atop the rail, using it for support. Shaking, he placed his crutches against it. His hospital issue, pale blue cotton gown wrapped lightly around his emaciated legs and billowed around his wasted body within the confines of a gray terrycloth robe. He reached deep into the robe's pocket and pulled out a small red-and-white pack. As I watched, he deftly shook loose the stick of tobacco. His gaunt face relaxed as he placed it between his parched lips. Straw-like fingers cupped the cigarette and lighter. Eyes closed, he inhaled deeply. At the approach of a stocky, robust young man walking energetically towards him, his eyes sparked in recognition and his tired face stretched into a welcoming grin.

Jack leaned in and whispered in my ear: "Poor guy; he doesn't have much longer." Jack's message was clear. On the edge of the Castro district, this hospital was well known for its treatment of patients with HIV and AIDS. Jack did not need to say more.

Taking the top two steps with his usual energetic leap, Jack's well-shined black leather shoes smacked the concrete solidly. As he moved on to fulfill his own agenda, I hesitated for a moment to watch the two friends hold each other in a warm, welcoming embrace. Jack's comment had evoked my feelings of sympathy and sadness, thinking of what lay ahead for them.

The steel-framed glass double doors of the hospital lobby slid apart with a whoosh and I shuddered when the warm air, tinged with a sense of escaping life, engulfed us. Jack reached for my arm and quickly guided me towards the gift shop. As I tried to shake off the image of the two men left behind on the veranda, I thought of Tom Hanks' portrayal in *Philadelphia*, and in particular, a song.

"Heaven please send to all mankind,
Understanding and peace of mind,
But if it's not asking too much,
Please send me someone to love."

"Someone to love," the haunting voice of Sade sang, as I remembered the sad Percy Mayfield melody.

Isn't love what all of us want? I thought.

"I want some Jujubes," Jack's voice intruded, as he deftly navigated us around a slow-rolling wheelchair. Pushing the gift shop door open, Jack headed for the only obstacle between himself and the bright green box dotted with yellow, orange, and red—a cashier who moved slowly to acknowledge the dollar bill he had placed on the counter.

"Thanks!" Jack said, picking up the small box of candy and waving it overhead. With another wave, he dismissed the change, leaving it on the counter. With his shoulder to the swinging door, he urged me through as he broke open the box.

We were quickly caught in the stream of mankind as it flowed down the hallway toward the hospital's elevator. "You want one?" Jack offered, as he shook a deep purple and a red Jujube into his open palm.

I extended my hand, smiling at the distraction, but as the rainbow-colored shapes dropped from the rectangular box, I was again reminded of the two men on the veranda.

"Let's go to Tower Records when we're done here! There's a new CD I want to get." He smiled at his idea, oblivious of my melancholy.

"What's it this time, Jack? Has Enya come out with a new CD?" I chided, as we stepped into the empty elevator. The sticky glob of candy made meaningful conversation difficult.

"No," Jack laughed. "It's a CD by the San Francisco Gay Men's Choir. One of my patients sings with the choir. I know I told you about him. I saw him today and he mentioned it came out last week. The choir will donate the proceeds to AIDS research." He jabbed the elevator button with a knuckle of the hand that was still holding tight to the box of Jujubes. "It's another way I can show my support," he said matter-of-factly.

"Besides – they're good!" he interjected enthusiastically, as the elevator bell sounded our floor. "Remember last year, about a week before Christmas, I heard caroling as I did my evening rounds? I'm sure I mentioned it," he said, not waiting for my answer. "It was the choir. It's become a holiday season tradition here. Their way of providing support and comfort to those who are ill during the holiday. Their voices were so moving. I will never forget that evening." I could see by Jack's saddened expression that their singing had touched him.

"The sound was eerily sweet, as if angels were singing." As he said this he glanced away, clearing his throat of emotion.

I envisioned the scene as Jack spoke. The harmony of the male voices as they walked the dimly lit hospital corridors, providing a lullaby for those about to go to sleep for the evening—or possibly forever—caused the sense of melancholy to wash over me again.

"I am sure there were some who thought they had died and gone to heaven!" Jack joked, though his attempt at dark humor felt out of place.

"Are you hungry?" Jack asked, changing the subject as we entered his office. "After, we'll stop and get something to eat at Orphan Andy's or Zuni."

"You mean the Jujubes weren't enough, Jack?" I teased, trying to follow his lead and lighten the mood, as I noted the slight, churning sensation of hunger in the pit of my stomach. Without answering, Jack had moved on, quickly taking a chart from his office manager, he began scribbling notes on a sheet of paper as she engaged him in conversation.

"Okay, as long as I can get home by seven," I said, more to myself. I made a mental note to call the sitter, and assure her that I would stop and pick up my younger two children, as we had agreed to earlier in the day.

After several phone calls and a goodnight to the office staff, Jack was ready to go.

"Keep in mind, Juanita, that if I had your body parts, I could have gotten the IT guy up here STAT to take care of that computer problem, too," Jack chided, as we started for the door.

"You're just jealous," Juanita responded.

"What was that about, Jack?" I asked after we left the office.

"It's nothing," he said, but his comment reminded me of the Sunday afternoon a few weeks before when Jack had sped his tiny red sports car across the Bay Bridge going seventy-five in the posted fifty-five mile-per-hour zone. Stopped by the Highway Patrol and given a ticket that promised a hefty fine, Jack had commented as we pulled back onto the freeway, "If I were a woman, I could have batted my eyes, and he would have let me go." His tone was angry and seemed tinged with envy.

"You're wrong about that Jack," I had said. "Being a woman doesn't give you a get-out-of-jail-free card."

We boarded the elevator and made the quick nonstop descent to the hospital lobby. It was dinnertime in the North Tower, and the halls were quiet.

Through large pane windows that faced west, I noticed the sun beginning to set and my attention was taken once again by the two men I had seen earlier embracing on the veranda. This time, they were moving in slow unison towards Jack and I through the lobby. The tall, fragile man placed the bulk of his weight on the crutches, his energy spent. Depending upon the supportive strength of his companion to steady him, he took short, halting steps, frequently stopping to muster his breath and the courage to continue.

Empathizing with him, I felt anger at his predicament. Before me was a man whose body was wasting away from a disease for which there was no known cure. His face, once tanned brown and shielded by the wide brim of a cowboy hat, was easily recognizable to America through TV and magazine ads. Now no one would recognize him. His strong angular features, square jaw and chiseled nose now appeared as a gaunt mask, accentuated by sunken eyes. A colorful plaid shirt decorated with flat pearl white buttons had once covered his muscular frame. Now, a pale blue cotton hospital gown covered his withered form. Moments from his life flashed before my eyes as he walked past.

As the lobby doors whooshed open, I took a moment to turn for a last look, with a deeply felt need to honor a life that would be too soon cut short. My memory of him would always be that of a ruggedly handsome man, strong hands holding reins tight, balancing astride a dark brown stallion on the crest of a hill. To me, he would always be the Marlboro Man.

Chapter 9

The Four-Letter Word

"So much for an afternoon away from work," Tara says, obviously irritated as she returns from taking her phone call. "Len hasn't been able to find the Jackson-Haley contract so I may have to go get a copy from the office and hand deliver it to him," Tara says, with a sigh of disappointment. "But, please, for now, go on. While I wait to hear back from him, tell me more."

Her short absence has given me time to think.

"Did I ever tell you about the Marlboro Man?" I ask.

"That great-looking guy in the ads?"

"There *were* several who played the part, but one named Christian Haren stood out for me," I say, as I give her a condensed version of what happened that day. "Seeing him and knowing that his future would be cut short, weighed heavily on my mind. As I sat having dinner at Orphan Andy's that evening, I looked across the table at Jack and thought, thank God, I am heterosexual, and in a monogamous relationship. I was relieved to know something like that couldn't happen to me."

"I certainly can relate," Tara acknowledges. "There is something to be said for being heterosexual and in a committed relationship—particularly in San Francisco!"

"Then, what comes next should interest you," I say, as I motion to the manuscript.

Tara picks it up and begins to read aloud.

"Holding tight to the still-sealed, small white envelope in my hand, I took a deep breath, unaware of the hard, cold surface of the concrete bench where I sat trembling—not from the cold, but from fear. I had to know."

"What's this, Diane?" Tara's brow furrows with a look of concern.

"Go back a couple of pages. Yes, start there," I say, hoping that by having her read it, I will not have to re-live those moments.

But as Tara reads, I cannot help but remember the heart-pounding fear that I felt as I sat on the concrete bench, stuck in an avoidance pattern, holding the small white envelope in my hand, while a voice inside my head urged, *open it*. And, how I had slowly slid my index finger along the envelope's edge, while avoiding reading its contents, as my mind flashed on the events that had led up to that day.

* * *

I stepped off the elevator onto the fourth floor and followed the directional blocks of blue-and-beige tile that I knew would eventually lead to Jack's office. I wondered, *why did he call?*

"I need to talk to you. Meet me at four o'clock." He had given no explanation, and the urgency in his voice left me feeling uneasy, so I hurried.

I could see Jack pacing at the far end of the hall. His arms were folded across his chest. He walked head down. *He looks stressed*, I thought. *What's troubling him?*

Crisply dressed in his black suit, he was the epitome of a professional. Against the background of an avocado green shirt, his tie-of-the-day was one he discovered at the Museum Company on the previous Sunday afternoon. I remembered his elation at finding the stained-glass pattern of a rose window on silk, and I couldn't help but smile and admire him. *He always looks sharp!*

The click of my high heels on the hard tile floor alerted him of my approach, and he looked up. I smiled, expecting a smile back, but was met with a tense, unsmiling Jack.

Something is wrong! But what?

"Got your message—Jack, are you okay?" I asked.

"Come here, Diane," he said, reaching for my arm and pulling me to his side. And in a lowered voice, he said, "I need to tell you something. But before I do, I need to know that no matter what happens you will still be my friend." His eyes demanded my confirmation and I realized he was serious!

"What are you talking about? Still be your friend?" I thought about how much *beyond* friends we had become and held back a laugh. "Jack, I *am* your friend."

Jack wasn't smiling. *Why would Jack say such a thing? He wasn't making any sense.* I realized again— he was dead serious.

"Jack, you're scaring me! Is something wrong?"

His facial expression showed his exasperation at my flurry of questions. His voice was nearly inaudible and squeaked when he spoke, as if he couldn't get the words out.

"I went to finalize my loan today, Diane. There's a problem."

I knew Jack had been watching his finances in preparation for buying a condo. "A place that is mine, a place I can call home," he had said. *How could he think his financial status would affect our relationship or my feelings for him?* My mind ran with it and raced

49

through scenarios that could be upsetting him, but nothing I could come up with made any sense.

"What kind of problem? They won't give you the loan?" I asked, not waiting for his response. "That's ridiculous!" I said, continuing in his defense. "But it's not the end of the world." I wanted to get him out of the mood he was in, to understand what was going on—to reassure him—and make it better.

"Surely it can be worked out," I added, "It can't be because you don't have the ability to repay it! So, what can the problem be? What can they be thinking?" Puzzled, I stopped my rant and waited for a response.

Jack had slumped back against the wall, his usual energy deflated. He stared at the floor and avoided my gaze.

"It's not that. Diane, I can get the loan," he said. "But there are provisions. As part of the loan stipulation, I am required to take out a life insurance policy, and *that* requires a physical." Clearing his throat, he began to speak slowly, distinctly. "When the results are in, I need to know you will still be my friend. That's all I am asking, Diane. Your friendship is important to me. I don't want to lose your friendship." Jack had turned pale.

"Jack, it will be okay!" I tried to reassure him. "I would think that an exam for this type of policy is routine. They just want to know you will live long enough to pay it back!" I laughed, and then caught myself.

"Jack, are you ill? What haven't you told me?"

"They want me to have an HIV test." He took a couple of steps back, to give himself distance.

I felt a sudden sense of relief—*he isn't ill!*

"Oh, Jack, seriously!" I laughed, "It just takes a couple of minutes. They draw the blood and you're out of there. It's no big deal. You of all people can't be afraid of needles!" I couldn't help but poke fun as I remembered his "Now relax, this is going to hurt you more than it's going to hurt me" mantra he gave to patients with a smile just before giving an injection. I waited for his acknowledgement, but no words came my way.

"I'm worried I'll test positive." His words hit. I fell back, and felt the blood drain from my face, as my mind tried to wrap itself around the implications of what he had said.

"Positive? That's not funny, Jack! You can't mean that. Why would you say such a thing?"

He remained silent.

He's serious! My voice choked in my throat. I felt the floor drop away and I grabbed for the wall. Jack caught me. "This can't be happening!" I stammered.

I barely heard his words over the pounding in my ears. *I can't breathe.* I gasped.

"I've never been tested!" His frantic voice blurted through my haze. "At times, I wanted to, but I could not bring myself to face the truth. I'm sorry, Diane."

"Truth! What are you saying? How? What happened? Needle sticks? How long have you thought you were positive, Jack?" I wanted a plausible explanation.

"You want the truth? No, Diane, not needle sticks."

"What then? Come clean, Jack! What! Are you telling me you've been seeing other women?" Then another possibility struck. "Prostitutes?" I recoiled, my voice raised in anger, as I thought of the six years we had been together. We were sexually exclusive! Weren't we?

"No, Diane. Not prostitutes. There's no one else. I'll tell you what happened, but please keep your voice down. Let me explain."

"Keep my voice down, Jack? How dare you ask me to keep my voice down?" My eyes burned with tears that would not fall. My hysteria came full circle. "You think you will test *positive*? You, of all people, *know* the seriousness of what you are saying! You have put *my* health at risk. I'm the mother of five children, Jack! They depend on me! You say you *may* be HIV positive! How long have you known this? Did you know before you slept with me the first time? When you said, 'Don't worry, I'm disease-free.' Or, later, Jack—two years later, when we decided we could have unprotected sex because we were exclusive?" Words came even faster. "Jack! How could you lie about something like this?"

"Diane please listen!" he implored.

"Listen to what? More lies, Jack? Did you know this past year when I told you I thought I was pregnant? Oh, Jack! How could you?"

"No, Diane, it's not what you think," he said. "Remember my telling you about the time I lived in New York? It was years ago." Jack's words rush out. "I'm sorry that I didn't tell you everything. I know I should have. It was the summer before I started college. I was a kid trying to figure out who I was and what I wanted, so I experimented. I wondered if I was bisexual. I went to bars, had a couple of one-night stands. That's it. But a couple of weeks after one encounter, I got sick."

"Jack! What? You were with men?" My mind spun out of control as his words sent me on a head-on collision course with death.

"I thought I had the flu. But when the AIDS epidemic became front page news, I began to worry that I may have been infected with HIV, had developed antibodies, and may have gone through what is called seroconversion, and that maybe the symptoms I had

52

were not from the flu at all. I consoled myself that I never developed further symptoms. Also, by this time, I had been married for a couple of years. My wife had an HIV test for her job, and her test came back negative." Jack paused, briefly monitoring my reaction. "I let myself believe that if she was okay, then so was I."

"So, you are saying you ignored it, Jack! Even knowing it was possible your wife could be immune, knowing everything you know about HIV, you ignored it?" My anger continued to build.

"I know. I was in denial, Diane. I wouldn't let myself think about it."

"I was okay when I met you, Jack. I got regular testing. I even showed you the lab results," I said. "I trusted you, and you lied to me, Jack!" Cold, shaking with shock, I wanted to run.

"How dare you ask me to be your friend? I don't even know you!" I screamed at him as I backed away. "Have your test, Jack, and I'll have one too. When the results come back, show me. I want to see the actual lab paper, Jack, whether it's positive, or negative," I said. "And I'll show you mine. Be your friend, Jack?" I said, disbelieving that friendship was his main concern.

As I turned and ran, I heard him whimper words that chased me down the hallway. "I'm sorry, Diane, but I was afraid!"

Chapter 10

Saved by the Bell

Tara takes a deep breath before looking me in the eye to ask, "Are you okay?"

I tell her about the trip to the lab, the two days it had taken to get the appointment, and how as I watched the vial fill with blood, I agonized over how I would tell my children if the results came back positive.

* * *

"All finished," said the robust, middle-aged female phlebotomist with matter-of-fact concern. "Don't worry, honey, it's all very confidential," she added, placing the special number identification sticker on the vial of my blood before she placed it into a special mailer.

"How soon can I expect the results?" I asked, wanting them yesterday.

"We don't run the test here. The results will come back to us in a sealed envelope from our off-site lab, which we hand over to you unopened," she stated. Sensing my state of mind, she reached out and gave my hand a gentle squeeze. "We will call you right away when the results come in, dear," she said in a motherly tone, leaving my question unanswered.

* * *

"The days dragged by. Tara, I can't tell you how anxious I was. I had picked up a Centers for Disease Control brochure in the waiting room and discovered that 84% of women in the U.S. that contract HIV get it from having heterosexual sex. Did you know that?"

"No, I didn't." Tara looks stunned. "Not needles, or drugs . . . but someone they trust?"

"Exactly. The information did not help my state of mind. The reality was that I needed to accept the fact that I could have contracted HIV. I began to re-plan my future. I suffered over how I would tell my children that their mother might not be around to see them grow up."

"I don't know what I would have done in your position. How long did it take before you got the results back?" Tara asks.

"A full two weeks," I say, remembering wanting, yet dreading the call.

"And?" asks Tara, now on the edge of her seat.

"After I got the call, I went to the lab immediately. The results were handed to me in a sealed envelope as promised. I remember how afraid I was to open it. I needed to go somewhere private."

Tara swallows her anticipation and lets me tell her in my own time.

"I thought about going into the hospital chapel, but chose the hospital's Rose Garden instead. Outdoors, quiet, I could sit down and cry, and not be seen. I realized I was facing the most difficult situation I had *ever* been in in my life. But it was one I could not avoid—I had to know. Knowing no one was around, I pulled the crisp white lab sheet from its envelope. My eyes scanned for the words that would hold the clue to my future. It read, "Test Result: HIV Negative.""

Chapter 11

Pandora's Box

"Thank God, Diane!" Tara says, as tension leaves her face and she sinks back into her chair. She quickly asks and answers her next questions in one statement.

"And, Jack—his results . . . you stayed?" Her voice echoes her disbelief. "Why?"

"It was one of those pivotal moments each of us have during our lives when we make a decision and hope it is the right one"

Not expecting Tara to understand, I decide to try to explain why anyway.

"Relieved and with a negative result in hand, I waited for Jack to call. I needed him to follow through. I hadn't spoken to him since I had given him the ultimatum. Had he gotten tested? I didn't know. He had carried the fear for so long. Had he been able to muster the courage to do what he needed to do for himself, and do right by me?"

"But he *did* call?" she asks.

"The next evening, I found him waiting for me next to my car when I got off work."

"Did he test negative? Did he show you the results as you asked?"

57

"Yes," I say, as I remember how Jack displayed his dot-matrix sheet like a trophy. "He looked apprehensive and apologetic and handed it to me before he hugged me, saying, 'I'm so sorry I put you through this. I'm so sorry.'"

"And you were okay with that?"

"Bottom line," I say. "When the results of the HIV test came back negative for both of us, I felt lucky and I rationalized reasons to stay."

"I don't know that I could have been as forgiving!" Tara states bluntly.

"As angry as I was at Jack's nondisclosure, knowing we were both well and healthy was such a relief that it took the edge off of my initial feeling of betrayal. I also remembered Jack's plea to remain his friend, and it bolstered a hope that his fear of losing me meant that we had a relationship he was serious about keeping. We had been together for six years, Tara! We had gone through so much. We had plans for the future. I thought that all of our secrets were out. We were okay. I let myself believe that we had been given a second chance."

I can tell, Tara isn't convinced.

"I think I understand your thoughts, Tara," I say, still defending my action. "At the time, I remember feeling that the experience had brought Jack and I closer together in a way that only facing life or death with someone can. At first, it seemed to make our relationship stronger."

"I understand where it might," Tara says, seeming to relent, accepting my explanation in a way I knew only a true friend would.

"But things began to change?" She raises the question.

"Yes. Initially, I thought we were doing fine," I say. "For myself, I focused on the quality time I could give to

58

my children. Jack saw it as an opportunity to give back. Grateful for his life, he looked into community programs where he might do good for others. He joined a hotline organization that gave free, confidential, and non-judgmental information about sex to anyone who called."

"And encouraged people at risk for HIV to get tested?" Tara bounces back.

"Exactly," I say, grateful that she gets it. "They promoted safe sex practices in the community, worked with young adults, and reached out to those on the fringe of society, such as sex workers."

Tara nods.

"Jack gave more and more of his time. From my perspective, it was almost as if Jack had taken a part-time job. He had a schedule that took a lot of his free time, time that began to cut into time we otherwise would have shared together."

"So you saw less of him?" Tara asks.

"Yes. Over the weeks that followed, he became more and more involved in what I believed were organization-led functions, like meetings and events. When I inquired, he explained that because of the confidential nature of the work, he could not discuss much of what went on."

"Sounds like you wanted to believe him, but weren't really sure if he was telling the truth."

"At first, I saw no reason not to believe him, but as time went on, I began to tire of his emergency meetings. I felt excluded from an important portion of his life. I sensed his defensiveness when I would ask questions. After a few weeks, I let him know I felt he had a secret life and confronted him about it."

"So, you worried there was someone else?"

"Yes," I answered, and remembered those unhappy confrontations.

"And?" Tara pursues.

"There is no one else, he would say. This is about me."

"Isn't that what they always say?" Tara's reaction borders on anger.

"That was my initial reaction. However, Jack explained that he was not only in a position to help the community at large, but that in the process he was making friends with co-workers. He had never had many friends and that now that he *was* making friends, he wanted to develop those relationships. You have your own friends, why I shouldn't have friends of my own?"

"What was I supposed to say? Of course, I encouraged his having friends, but Jack seemed not to grasp my underlying point. He knew all of my friends and they accepted him into their circle. But I wondered, was it his friends, or, by his own choice, that I was *not* being included? No matter what I said, he didn't seem to hear it."

"Oh, Diane, I'm sorry." The look on Tara's face shows me she understands.

"But that wasn't all. During one of these discussions, he said that he always felt he wore a mask, and that he could never be himself."

"Don't we all feel that way sometimes?" Tara asks.

"Of course, but for Jack, it seemed to go much deeper. He said he had never fit in. As a child he had been small and suffered bullying by other boys. He told me about a pet tortoise named Slow Poke that his parents got for him when he was four years old. It was his oldest companion. Jack smiled when he told me the tortoise became large enough to ride. It roamed around on a chain in his backyard. With no close friends, Slow Poke was everything to him."

"What a wonderful experience for a child!" Tara's reaction is as I expect.

"His smile dissolved as he told me how one of the boys who bullied him came to his home one weekend while he was away with his parents and strangled the tortoise with its chain. He wept as he related the story, and I understood the incident had caused him deep pain."

"Oh, Diane, that's so unimaginably cruel," says Tara, looking horrified.

"It didn't stop there, though," I say, remembering Jack's comments about other situations. "He said he couldn't be *himself* and find acceptance, stating that as he got older, he wasn't athletic like the other boys and that activities such as sports, held no interest for him. He saw boys as intimidating and he didn't like them; girls weren't interested in him . . . he wasn't popular. He also stated that even his parents were ashamed of him!"

"He said that?"

"I was surprised too," I say. "It was one of the few times Jack spoke about his family."

"Diane, what made him say such a thing!"

"I asked him the same thing, unable to fathom that his parents were ashamed of him. Then, he gave me the example of a time when his mother had her woman friends over for a coffee klatch. He was about fifteen. He had come home from high school, and as he walked into the kitchen, and with the women sitting around the table, Jack said his mother stated sarcastically to her friends, 'Oh, look, here comes my little girl.'"

"What? Diane, how humiliating! What mother would tease her child like that?"

"Apparently, his did." I say. "But after hearing his story, I didn't want to say much to him about his work with the organization, or the time it took from us. I only wanted to help him erase some of his pain, and help him to enjoy the experience of having friends in his life."

"So, you let it go?"

"I did," I say with a nod. "And, Jack vowed to give *us* the time we needed. So again, I felt we were okay. I was happy that we were communicating and that Jack was willing to share things about himself. You know how it is. When you have been with someone for a long time, you get comfortable and tend to feel that you know everything there is to know about them, but you become more attached when such revelations are shared."

Tara laughs. "That happens, doesn't it?"

I pick at the piece of tiramisu that had come with my lunch and reach for a glass of water. My throat was dry from talking.

"What I didn't know, was that I would soon discover that there was much more about Jack that he had not shared with me—or anyone else."

"What made me think you might say that?" Tara chuckles, knowing that the story was not over.

I sip the water slowly.

"What happened?" Tara asks.

"Jack got the loan and purchased a beautiful condo off of Divisadero in Pacific Heights. It was a gorgeous Victorian. It had a spectacular view of the bay from a room that Jack had quickly designated as the formal dining room." As I speak, I picture how Jack kept the room sparsely furnished with only a small round table, and on one wall had hung a stately wall tapestry of *The Unicorn in Captivity*, a beautiful piece, which he had purchased in New York at the Metropolitan Museum of Art.

"There was a pillow-tufted window seat that curved its way along the base of the enormous window. I remember blissfully watching a barge inch its way under the Golden Gate, as Jack read the *Chronicle* and sipped coffee. It was one of those perfect together moments when all was right with the world. Then I asked, "Would you like to do something special for your birthday, Jack?"

"His birthday?" Tara smiles.

"Jack hadn't talked much about his upcoming big 5-0. It felt like a good time to broach the subject."

How wrong I was, as I remembered our conversation of that morning.

* * *

"I can throw a party for you, or we can take a trip," I said, knowing how much Jack liked the idea of seeing new places. We can drive up the coast towards Mendocino. Maybe stay at Sea Ranch—you've always wanted to go there. What do you think? We can go wherever you like, Napa Valley or, maybe Big Sur? Think of it. Quiet—no pagers, great food, cute little shops. We haven't been to Vegas!" I added, hoping to see some glimmer of interest at any suggestion."

"I don't even want to think about my birthday, Diane!" Jack had answered curtly, without looking up. His response was tinged with anger and he was resolute. He kept his nose buried in the paper in an effort to ignore me."

"Jack! You need to celebrate! Think about it!" I babbled on. "Nowadays, fifty is only half a lifetime! You're healthy and your finances are good; you're much better off than most. Chances are we will both live to be one hundred! So why not think of it that way? Or, think of it like this. You're fifty, so you have fifty more years to live. What are you going to do with *those* fifty years? Instead of dwelling on time gone by, why not plan to use the next fifty years to do something that you have always wanted to do?"

Jack stopped pretending to read and looked up. There was a look on his face I had never seen before. He put the paper down and rose from the window seat. His bare feet padded softly over the dark oak floor as he paced in several large circles, with his arms crossed and shoulders hunched, deep in thought. I realized I had awakened something within him. He stood for several moments then walked over and seemed to study the tapestry. Finally, he turned and looked out the window towards the sea.

"You might be right, Diane," he said. "You might be right."

Little did I know that my question was the key that would open Pandora's Box.

Chapter 12

Walking the Edge of the Abyss

"He told you what he wanted for his birthday?" Tara pushes. "I take it that what he wanted wasn't something you expected?"

"To say the least."

How do I tell Tara that I wondered if I had somehow given Jack the permission he needed to pursue what came next?

"Tara what do you know about kink?" I ask pensively, deciding I should build up to it.

She looks perplexed. "Kink—as in . . ."

"BDSM," I say, filling in the gap.

"BDSM . . . k-i-n-k, as in kinky?" Tara's eyes grew even wider. "Diane, you're referring to bondage and submission—S&M—sadomasochism?" Tara makes no effort to try to hide her surprise. "Sorry, I didn't see that one coming!"

"How could you have," but let me explain. There is an organization here in the city that is the West Coast's version of New York's infamous Eulenspiegel Society. Have you ever heard of The Eulenspiegel Society?"

Still shaking her head no, I can tell by her raised eyebrows, she is wondering what this had to do with Jack's birthday.

"Neither had I, but I soon learned that both are non-profit BDSM organizations that support sexual freedom. In a safe, non-exploitive environment, they provide education and support for people who want to explore their dominant and submissive natures."

"You *are* talking about S&M, as in kinky sex, whips and chains?" Her smile shows she is making fun, but I can sense there are questions forming.

"I am pretty sure I know what you are thinking," I counter. "BDSM is out of bounds, in a normal society. We both know the taboo that society has placed on S&M. There are common stereotypes around it—you just mentioned some of them, but the truth is, if you were to ask people, most would say they view themselves either as a dominant or a submissive personality. Think about it. In daily life, these roles are played out every day between people in different ways."

I can see that Tara is still wondering what it has to do with Jack and I, so I quickly continue.

"There are psychological, emotional, and spiritual aspects that individuals explore by role-playing."

"Are you trying to convince me that this is therapy, Diane?" Tara smiles dubiously.

I laugh. "Experienced S&M practitioners warn against utilizing S&M as therapy. But it can be very therapeutic."

"I am still not sure that I understand, Diane. What did this have to do with Jack? Did he want kinky sex for his birthday?" She had jumped right to the point.

"Not really," I say, as I remember how Jack ambled off to the kitchen for another cup of coffee, leaving me to wonder, *what was he thinking?* Then, when he came back coffee in hand, he led me to his study where he sat down in front of the computer, entered his password, and clicked his way to the local organization's website, before pulling me onto his lap.

66

With his arms around me, and disarmingly apologetic, he said, "I have been putting this off, but yet wanting to talk to you. I wasn't sure how to start the conversation. Here, read this."

"Tara, what Jack finally admitted was that he felt he was a submissive at heart and he wanted to explore that side of himself."

"What?" she exclaims.

"I know. I didn't know what to say either, my mind raced to conclusions. I heard S&M, and thought sex and porn, but Jack insisted the organization was educational. It wasn't about pornography, but about self-exploration in a safe, non-exploitive environment with like-minded people. For some it was about sex, but for others it was more about testing personal limits. He said it wasn't swinging, or partner swapping because he knew I wouldn't be okay with that. When he started talking about being a submissive, I really didn't know what he meant, but I did know my first hurdle was to get past my pre-conceived ideas and *listen*."

"That was how he wanted to mark his fiftieth birthday? Explore his submissive side through BDSM?" Tara looks incredulous.

"That's pretty much how I took it. It was unexpected, for sure."

"And you were okay with it?" Tara interjects again, still looking at me with surprise.

"At that moment, no." I remembered feeling horrible, stomach-knotting discomfort as he scrolled through their website, showing me snapshots of scene play. "Quite honestly, all I could think was, *what in hell is Jack thinking?* But what was I *supposed* to say? I only had preconceived ideas. *We are adults*, I thought. I felt I needed to be fair and hear him out. He confessed that he had attended a couple of events with people in the volunteer group. My mind went to recent times when Jack had canceled our plans last minute, and I wondered if attending the events were the cause. It was evident these experiences had been important to him and by what he said his interest didn't seem unhealthy"

"So, what did you do?" Tara asks.

"What *could* I do? I set my feelings aside. I was relieved that he had confided in me. I knew he was nervous and afraid of my reaction, as beads of sweat had formed on his forehead as he spoke. I thought if it was that important to him, perhaps I should set my fears aside and make the effort to understand. Between you and me, I needed to find out if it was something that was going to affect our relationship."

I take another sip of water, and think of the first time Jack kissed me—the look on his face had left me confused. Now, it had taken on new meaning.

"And?" Tara asks.

"Another thing to explore together—a new experience," I admit. "I took the challenge."

Chapter 13

Ties that Bind

"Taking on this new challenge meant active participation in a community that was foreign to anything I had ever known." I confide to Tara. "I had no idea what to expect. Jack told me that they offered an orientation that would give me an opportunity to meet members and ask questions, and he urged me to go."

"So you could find out what you were getting into?" Tara asks.

"Yes, I was able to speak to members and ask why they were there."

"And?" Tara continues to quiz.

"It was eye-opening. The people I met seemed to be searching for ways to expand and learn more about themselves and explore their psyche by testing personal boundaries. At orientation, I learned basic rules of safe, sane, and consensual S&M scene-play. As I understood more about the ways individuals used their BDSM experience, I began to see how it could have value for some people. Another important aspect, to me anyway, was that the organization insisted on honoring the privacy of its members. Members introduced themselves on a first-name-only basis or had a pseudonym, even a step further, you signed an agreement to protect the privacy of the members by not acknowledging them if you recognized them outside of organizational activities."

"In other words, you don't say hi if you run into someone on the street?" Tara gets it.

"Exactly," I said. "It was designed to protect members from the stereotype associated with S&M."

"What did you do?"

"It was inexpensive to join and by doing so, I could attend classes."

"You joined the organization and took classes?" Tara seems astonished.

"I hoped that by knowing more about S&M, I would understand what meaning it held for Jack. The most common activity was scene-play, acting out a pre-determined, or negotiated fantasy with another person. Usually, one plays the dominant, the other the submissive. It was a way for people to test boundaries and personal limits."

"Negotiated?" Tara asks.

"Yes. The scene to be acted out was discussed and agreed upon before being played. Safe words and rules were established. No scene was to continue if either party said no, or red, which was code for stop. For myself, I thought dressing up and acting out a part would be fun. While I wasn't sure what being a submissive *really* meant to Jack, I hoped to learn more by visiting some of the community *play* venues with him. And more importantly, in going, what might be Jack's expectation of *me*? Could I meet it? If so, could I live with it? That's what I really needed to find out."

"I had taken several classes and I had learned about a members-only play spot called The Castle. I sensed it was a safe place. As a newbie, I understood it would be trial and error. While I didn't want to make a

70

fool of myself, I felt I needed to prove myself, not only to myself, but to Jack. That I was ready to undertake this new scenario in our relationship, and while I had involved myself in some class participation, Jack and I had never played a scene together, not even in private. He would say I wasn't ready."

"Meaning, *he* wasn't ready?" Tara says.

"Or, perhaps he wasn't ready with *me*! Jack let it slip that he had gone to The Castle with the volunteer group. Of course, I couldn't help but wonder who he might have done scene-play with, but I didn't ask. I knew about Power Exchange, the public venue downtown and had gone inside with Jack one time, just to look. I had heard members say that there were three or four private S&M play-houses around the city, but within the S&M community, the invitation only events at The Castle were the ones they favored. Jack's enthusiasm at his own experience there had piqued my curiosity and I convinced myself that I wanted to go to The Castle with him."

"And?"

"I pushed until he finally relented. We discussed the possibility of playing a scene together if it felt right. I told him only if I took the dominant role and he agreed."

"I knew that some of things they had talked about in meetings, like piercings, or pain and humiliation, wasn't something that interested me. But what interested Jack? Jack always seemed to want to control his surroundings, so to me he wasn't a submissive personality. But I was beginning to wonder what else about Jack I didn't know. He talked very little about what he had seen and didn't tell me what he expected. I knew I was testing the water, but I needed to find out what was at the root of his interest in S&M."

"Weren't you nervous?"

"Extremely. Not only was I going with Jack, but we would play it out in public. In the community public play was an expectation. I had only gone through the motions in class. One member, who I will call Black Hawk, had been interested in playing a scene with me outside of class. That he was willing, had helped my confidence for sure. But I had said no. But for me, the real motivation was that I needed to show Jack I could play the dominant me over the submissive him. I also needed to know if it was something I could handle going forward."

"Makes sense to me," Tara says. "So what happened? Tell me about The Castle."

Chapter 14

The Castle

"The Castle was located downtown, off of 8th and Mission. I remember the evening like it was yesterday, and in particular, what I had to do to prepare for it. It was important to look the part, I couldn't afford to get expensive leather costumes or the thigh-high boots, I concentrated on the least expensive accessory—makeup. I highlighted my eyes with black liner, smoky dark shadow and thick black mascara. I chose a dark, blood-red lipstick and outlined my lips with an even darker shade. The colors popped, I looked very theatrical."

"You went with the Goth look?" Tara says.

"It seemed appropriate," I laugh.

"What *do* you wear to something like that?"

"Four-inch, silver-studded black stilettos I found in a cheesy shop in the Haight," I recalled teetering off-balance as I looked over my shoulder to check to see if the seams of my stockings were straight. "I found black fishnet stockings in a lingerie shop, and a very short, black spandex skirt at Buffalo Exchange. Frederick's of Hollywood supplied a one-piece teddy with long sleeves. It was black, sheer, and edged with lace. It turned out to be a perfect choice. Packaged, I didn't look too slutty. I had a jacket of soft black leather in my closet that I'd had for a long time. I wore it over my shoulders, but of course, I still needed to have a toy bag.

"A *what*?" Tara asks.

"Something to carry all of the equipment in. Things I thought might be useful in a scene based on what others had told me."

"Such as?" Tara asks curiously.

"An interesting array of items, everything from clothespins to feathers. I picked up a couple of items at Stormy Leather, including an inexpensive flogger made of soft suede, and went to Guitar Center and picked up a full handset of metal guitar picks I had seen one of the dominants use in class. I also took the graduation present Black Hawk had made for me as an enticement to play a scene with him—a flogger of tiny metal beads that hung in multiple strands from a wooden handle."

"That one sounds scary." Tara laughs as she cringes.

"It *looked* scary. I couldn't see myself ever using it, but it was fun to have in the toy bag. Jack retrieved the bag from the back seat of the car, and as I made my last-minute make-up touch-ups, he waited—like a good submissive should!" I mocked.

"An old warehouse housed The Castle in a dark alley off of Mission Street. I remember pulling down on the hem of my way-too-short skirt as we walked hurriedly, passed vagrants cloaked in shadows."

"Not the safest place at night?" Tara assumes correctly.

"No," I say remembering the seedy neighborhood. "Jack rapped twice on an unmarked metal door. It barely opened, a wedge of light shining through the crack. The beat of techno pulsed and spilled into the alley.

74

* * *

"Guest list?" a deep voice asked from a leather-hooded face. Curious eyes penetrated the mask's eye slits.

"Yes," Jack said, giving our pseudonyms. Then the door banged shut and we were left in the dark silence of the narrow alley.

Finally, the door re-opened and the Door Master allowed us to slip into the dimly lit interior. He wore only a torso harness and a leather jock strap on his heavy-set frame. We followed as he lumbered down a narrow corridor and led us through a curtained doorway into a brightly lit reception area. As I blinked to adjust to the light, I saw a woman with an overly ample bust, tightly corseted in a black leather bustier, sitting at a small table. She greeted us with an I-could-care-less look.

"Have you attended one of our events before?" she questioned, tossing a black feather boa around her neck.

"Yes and, no," Jack replied, nodding towards me.

"Read and sign," she commanded, handing me a waiver form. Her eyes were on the two twenty-dollar bills that Jack extended, and she deftly replaced the bills with a safe, sane and consensual statement before bidding us a good evening and taking my signed waiver.

The reception area was crowded and noisy, and Depeche Mode's *Master and Servant* played loudly in the background. There were folding tables set with chips, cookies, French rolls, and a variety of meats and cheeses on a large platter. A sign indicated food, sodas, and water were free; "*Wine, $3 a glass*" was written in black Sharpie on an index card on a table next to bottles of merlot and chardonnay. A man of slight build and downcast eyes, dutifully poured wine

75

and collected crumpled dollars from a thin, gray-haired woman in a tight black vinyl body suit. What really took me by surprise was that Catwoman appeared to be at least seventy. Interestingly, both men and women roamed the reception area, looking at each new person who entered as if hoping to connect with someone with whom they might share an evening of fantasy. If I hadn't been there with Jack, I would have felt very uncomfortable.

"Shall we explore?" Jack had shouted over the din of voices and music. Without waiting for my answer, he had started for a narrow stairway that led up to another level. Upstairs there were three dimly lit rooms decorated as medieval dungeons. One small room held only a St. Andrew's Cross and a wooden bench. In a much larger room were two metal cages, one large and one small, and two wooden racks for medieval torture. Suspension devices for bondage play hung from the ceiling and were attached to the walls. Both rooms were empty. However, on entering the third room, a chill went through me when I heard a voice plead from an aperture on a man-sized, mummy-shaped, metal box complete with metal loops on which to place a padlock, "Let me out! Please, master, let me out!"

No one was around. His master had gone into another room and left him. The lid was closed, and there was no padlock attached to the metal loops. But, I wondered, *does he know that?* My feeling was that he didn't.

I said to Jack: "There is someone in that metal coffin!"

"Of course," Jack replied. "It's all about mind-fuck." I realized Jack's answer showed no sign of empathy.

Well, it's working, I thought to myself, as I tried to come to grips with the thought of someone actually being locked inside. I started for the stairs, not waiting to see if Jack followed. In the reception area, I retrieved a cold can of Coke from the submissive with downcast eyes, hoping the soda's sparkle would wash away my feeling of uneasiness.

Jack caught up to me and took my hand, before leading me through a door into a large dimly lit room filled with tension and heat. I remember that the loud music pulsed in synchrony to the pounding of my heart. Colored lights tracked the large open space in a dizzying pattern. Again, adjusting to the light, my eyes pierced dark recesses where couples played with their partners and groups performed scene play for gawking onlookers. The voyeurs watched, at times chided, often asking if they could join in, but mostly just acted amused. "Slaves" were being auctioned on a stage in the center of the room.

An Asian woman tied in intricate rope bondage stood expressionless with a ball gag in her mouth while her male dominant offered to sell her to the highest bidder. I wasn't sure who was enjoying it more, the slave or her master. I felt it was more an exhibition than an auction.

In another corner, a female dominant dressed as a mommy, disciplined her male submissive baby brat, a man in his fifties, dressed in a baby's garb. Sitting in a child's playpen, the middle-aged man threw his oversized baby bottle at her. No one seemed to be paying any attention, including his mommy. I guess it was as Jack had said—all about mind-fuck.

The most fascinating scene I saw, though, was two lesbian dominants performing a ritualistic piercing of a man, his chest and genitals.

After placing a vinyl covering over the table he lay on, they pierced him with straight needles. In sharp contrast to the tension and discomfort evident on the faces of those who watched, the *victim* displayed a countenance of relaxed calm, seeming to enjoy his state of endorphin-induced euphoria.

Jack led the way, pushing past a voyeur who sat watching from a harness swing, and opened yet another door. "I haven't been back here before" Jack confessed.

As the door opened, I felt like I had fallen down the rabbit hole into the domain of Alice in Wonderland. This room was much smaller, square with a high-beamed ceiling. Three of its walls were painted lacquer black and one was painted a bright crimson red. The floor was covered in large black and white linoleum squares set in a harlequin pattern. Rose-colored light bulbs cast an eerie, pink glow. The combination of color and pattern gave the room a surrealistic feel. The furniture consisted of an overly-large four-poster bed with a mattress wrapped in red vinyl. The head of the bed was up against one of the shiny black walls. Next to the bed was a wooden bondage chair equipped with shackles. While a man and a woman coupled on the vinyl-covered bed, they seemed oblivious to three men that stood a distance away, talking and watching. No one seemed to care that Jack and I had entered the room, but I was a woman on a mission, so I did my best to ignore them. My attention instead went to the red wall. I recognized it as a warehouse drop-down door complete with six-inch diameter circular brass rings. Remembering what I carried in my toy bag, I saw potential in playing the scene with Jack. Because it was off the beaten path, it also gave me an added sense of comfort that it allowed us privacy.

"Jack," I whispered. "Would you be willing to do a scene with me here?" I felt myself challenge my own self-consciousness.

"Here?" he questioned, looking nervously around at the couple on the bed and at the voyeurs.

"Here," I said. "This room is the most quiet and out-of-the-way in the building. There, I pointed, against that red wall. We'll be quiet and they won't know we're here."

Chapter 15

The Red Wall

"What did he say?" Tara asks.

"Okay, sure," Jack said, giving in and setting the toy bag down on a small white leather ottoman that caused me to think again of Alice and the White Rabbit.

* * *

"Strip to the waist, Jack," I directed with a sudden show of confidence.

I wondered if he would balk and play the role of a submissive brat?

While Jack removed his clothes, I went through the toy bag and found what I wanted to use.

"Jack, kneel before me, then, place palms up on your thighs," I instructed.

"Yes, Mistress," he responded, without hesitation. He knelt at my feet in a submissive position.

He called me Mistress. So far, so good, I thought.

"Close your eyes and keep them closed," I commanded. "Don't speak until I give you permission. Remain in this position until I say otherwise." He did as I directed. In truth, I was surprised. A part of me had expected Jack *would* play the brat.

I went to the toy bag and removed a black blindfold. "Keep your eyes closed," I reminded him. I placed the blindfold over his eyes. "It will be green for continue, yellow for time out, and red for stop." I whispered the safe words we had agreed upon. "Do you understand? You may answer, Jack."

"Your wish is my desire, Mistress," Jack replied. He had begun to tremble.

"You're shaking. Are you cold?" I asked.

"No, Mistress," Jack said. "I am not cold. I am anticipating your desire."

"Stand up," I said, as I steadied him. "Turn around, walk three steps forward. You will stand against the red wall."

"On reaching the wall, I had Jack spread his arms and helped him grasp a brass ring in each hand. I withdrew red ribbon from the toy bag and ceremoniously bound his wrists tight to the brass rings, with easy-to-release knots. I took other toys from the bag, placing them within close reach.

"Are you ready to begin?' I asked Jack.

"I am ready, Mistress," he answered.

I was comfortable with sensation play—that is 'no-pain' or 'anticipation' play. I ran the tips of my fingers along the bare skin of his back and used my fingernails to trace wide and small patterns of line and circle on his freckled skin. I used feathers and fabrics of different textures and left traces of sensation along his back and arms . . . whispers of touch, my hands in constant motion.

Jack's breathing deepened to a relaxation state as the different objects provided unexpected sensations uniquely their own, while they were moved across his chest and abdomen in light, rhythmic patterns in a continued ebb and flow of touch. The idea was to raise sensual awareness and bring the mind in to center on the next pleasurable caress.

When I sensed by Jack's body language that he was nearing the endorphin high, I reached for the soft leather flogger and with a resounding *slap, Slap, SLAP*, I let it fall across Jack's back.

Jack drew a quick breath in surprise. *Perhaps he was beginning to wonder what was to come?*

"Green, Jack," I teased after repeating the motion several more times, not waiting for an answer. He sighed.

The flogger tails snapped against the already pink-tinged skin of his back, again and again, with light but firm, rhythmic smacks. Small welts appeared, as I increased the intensity. Jack did not flinch, but his knuckles blanched as his hands held the brass rings tight.

"Red, Jack?" I asked, as I monitored his physical state.

"No, Mistress," he said, breathing hard.

How far do I take this? I wondered.

The constancy of the flogging had set his endorphins in motion. His body was creating a mind high. The skin on Jack's back was pink, and warm to the touch. With planned precision, the flogging gave way to a neuro-wheel, its icy-cold points of steel tracing a sensation of needle-tipped pins across his sensitive skin. I watched the muscles of his back tense and quiver as he continued to climb the endorphin high. Placing a metal guitar pick on each of my fingers, I allowed their cold, pointed tips to trail along the peaks and valleys of his body, always aware of Jack's breathing as it quickened with a touch that barely skimmed his skin. Circles wide, then small, in unceasing rhythm crossed his back, shoulders, chest and abdomen.

"Yellow?" I questioned, but Jack made no sound. I knew the timing was right.

I shed the guitar picks, and reached forward, grasping his erect nipples, and pulled and bit into them with my fingernails. Jack moaned, shuddered, and began to break into a sweat.

"Red," I called without warning in Jack's ear, and I promptly ended the scene. He swayed and leaned against the cold surface of the crimson red door as I pulled loose the slipknots of the red ribbons that held his wrists. When I removed the blindfold from his eyes, he slipped to his knees, shaking, at my feet.

"Thank you, Mistress," he gasped.

I had completed the scene and to my surprise, Jack had followed all of my instructions. This gave me a great sense of satisfaction, as well as relief, but did it mean I had proven myself to Jack? *Time will tell*, I remembered thinking.

I turned to retrieve the toy bag, and it was then I saw that the room was overflowing with men and women. Each had quietly come in to the room, crushing together to watch us play our scene. They had been careful to leave enough space behind me so that I could work undisturbed. With my back to the door, and fully focused on Jack, I had been unaware of their presence. Seeing them standing there, I suddenly realized that all of the effort I had put into making the evening work, just to prove something to Jack, had taken an unexpected turn. Whether I proved myself to Jack or not, I had achieved more than I had have anticipated. By their silence, it was clear that I had gained the respect of a community.

Chapter 16

Rules of the Game

"Their reaction must have fueled your confidence," Tara says. "How did Jack react?"

"It certainly did," I agree. "The evening proved to be the start of a turning point."

"How so?" Tara asks.

"I had proven I could play the game, but I still didn't know what all of it meant to Jack or how it was supposed to work on a personal level for us. He did not criticize me, which I half expected. I wondered if he didn't say anything because we had drawn so much attention that evening. I also thought he might still be trying to figure it out for himself. To my surprise, Black Hawk called me the next afternoon. He had heard from another member about the scene I had done with Jack."

"Oh, so now you have a following?" Tara chuckles.

I laugh. "Black Hawk had asked before if I would do a scene with him. You will remember that I said no . . ."

"Because you were only doing it to connect with Jack, I remember. So how did it become a turning point?" Tara asks.

"Black Hawk was a sweet guy. He'd been helpful and taught me things. Once he took me to Home Depot after a class, and explained about safety release hooks and how to tie knots. Then he had given me the metal bead flogger he made as a special gift."

"He knew the ropes," Tara chuckles at her own humor.

"Yes, he did. But he knew I was with Jack. Still, I felt I owed him for all he had done to help me."

"What did you do?"

"I decided to take him up on his offer. He wanted to go to Power Exchange, the public venue downtown that I had avoided. My confidence was up or I would have said no. I agreed to go the next Friday evening, just for practice, or so I thought."

"Power Exchange. I thought you weren't sure about going to a public place," Tara says.

"And I should have followed my gut," I replied.

* * *

It was a pitch-dark night and it had been difficult to find parking along Harrison Street. Black Hawk was of a stature and attitude that made me feel safe, but I had a sense of relief as he pushed open the metal door of Power Exchange, and we entered the popular downtown sex club.

I waited, listening to the pulse-pounding techno music as Black Hawk paid our entrance fee to an attractive woman with long red hair. I noticed two women standing inside a small anteroom, almost blocking a narrow but well-lit hallway that I knew led in a serpentine fashion throughout the first floor. They were jeering at the single men who came through the entrance and asked each if they wanted a flogging. I didn't recognize either of them as dominants from the S&M community, and it occurred to me that they could be prostitutes. The thought made me feel uneasy.

I knew from the walk-through of Power Exchange with Jack that each floor had several small mini-dungeon play rooms with doors that players could close so as not to be disturbed. Each door had a small window so that house monitors could do a safety check and view, and curious others could watch the scene being enacted while standing in the hallway. There was no privacy.

The rooms were sparsely decorated with just a chair, a table, and some piece of basic bondage equipment such as a harness swing or a St. Andrew's Cross. How the equipment was used depended upon one's imagination and, ultimately, whatever the dominant brought along in his or her toy bag.

I had cleaned and repacked my equipment after The Castle event. Before we got out of the car, Black Hawk had handed me a pair of leather handcuffs, which I stuffed into my bag and he asked if I had remembered my safety release hooks. I had—I was ready. After purchasing a couple of bottles of water, we walked up a stairwell papered in black felt covered with planets and stars which glowed neon under black light, and searched for a room away from the general public foot traffic.

We found a small well-lit room with a high ceiling. Two wooden beams traversed one corner of the small room from one wall to the other. One dropped down about three feet from the ceiling and the other was placed six inches above floor level. Each beam had several four-inch circular metal ring attachments. A straight-backed wooden chair had been pushed up against one wall. A nearby shelf held lube, a box of condoms, a large roll of paper towels, a box of latex gloves, a large bottle of Purell, and other miscellaneous items. I took off my coat and hung it on a coat hook on the wall. I had worn a black, faux leather corset, a black, too-short miniskirt, and the same four-inch silver-studded stilettos and fishnet stockings I had worn to The Castle. While I finished checking out the room, Black Hawk removed his clothing down to a leather jockstrap. Then, without my asking, he kneeled on the concrete floor in front of me.

We negotiated the scene in the usual way, agreeing on safe words. Green was for resume, yellow for continue with caution, and at Black Hawk's request, we substituted black for red. It would mean a moment's rest at My Lady's discretion. He was an experienced player, so I knew he wanted me to push his limits. It was particularly important in public play to follow the rules of safe, sane, and consensual scene play to reflect the community's guidelines. I trusted he knew his limits, and I knew he wanted to push mine. I knew 'black' was his way of letting me know he would not call 'red' and the scene would only end if *I* was ready to end it. *But was I up to the test?*

"Are you ready to begin?" I asked.

"If it pleases My Lady," Black Hawk answered.

I placed the leather hood that Black Hawk had asked me to use, over his head and slowly zipped it closed. It only had openings only for the nostrils, mouth, and ears, Black Hawk shivered in anticipation. I ordered him to stand with his back to the door, facing the corner. I placed the leather handcuffs around his wrists and leather ankle cuffs around his ankles. His arms were spread wide with his hands over his head. Attaching the safety release hooks to each handcuff, I connected each to the circular metal rings on the wood beam above him. I had him spread his legs in a position that would support his body, before securing the set of ankle cuffs to the lower wooden beam. He had asked that I not share with him what I planned, so once he was ready and waiting, I began to remove items from my toy bag.

I started out much like I had with Jack, with my fingers slowly tracing lightly over his body, beginning with the back of his arms, working down and over the muscles of the back, buttocks, and legs. I was a novice, and no match for his experience, so I was surprised to see his apparent vulnerability. I guessed that he was excited that I was willing to do a scene with him. I took it slow, and watched his body react—his muscles tightening as I ascended the front of his body and slowly moved my hands upward, being careful not to touch his private parts.

I used fingertips first, and then exchanged fingertips for rabbit fur, rabbit fur for feathers, feathers for wisps of silken fabric, and finally anything I could find in my toy bag that would give different physical touch sensations to the skin. I moved across his body rhythmically and predictably, always to heighten the crescendo of sensation. Without breaking stride, I followed up by using the black suede flogger and began to lightly swipe its tails across his back, quickening the rhythm with more solid blows: *smack, smack, SMACK!* As I increased intensity, pink stripes appeared on his skin. After several minutes, his rhythmical breathing deepened as he hit the endorphin high, and tiny beads of sweat glistened on his chest and began to run down his neck from beneath the hood. I leaned my full body against his and whispered my offer in his ear, "Red—or black?"

"Black, if it pleases My Lady," he whispered hoarsely, as he swayed against his restraints.

A little surprised, I realized that when the endorphins are triggered, the submissive is on a body high and feels euphoric. That's when the dominant must be watchful. You don't want to let it go too far; the sub is usually in a body state and a mind state of charged vulnerability. But done right it also can enrich someone's experience. I reached for the flogger with the strands of metal beads Black Hawk had made for me.

"I have something for you," I said, as I dragged its icy tails across his reddened skin.

He arched his back and began to shiver. He would know what it was, and I was counting on the psychological implication to be enough. Suddenly, I heard the door behind me move as those standing in the hallway pushed against it. Then I heard a voice cry, "Look! It's Diane!"

Startled and caught off guard, I turned and caught a glimpse of several men outside the door, each straining to look through the window. I didn't recognize anyone, but I realized someone had recognized me and wasn't following the rules. I was distracted and dismayed at being called out in this public place.

I reached for the waist of Black Hawk's leather jock strap and called "yellow," pulling him gently back to his standing position. Then, without further word, I reached around his body and grasped and squeezed his erect nipples. He moaned, and again swayed against the confines of the cuffs that held him.

"You please me greatly," I whispered in his ear. "Your Lady is very pleased." I placed my hands on his waist to steady him, and I whispered, "We are finished for tonight."

"Thank you, My Lady," he whispered as I watched his body relax. "Thank you."

I released Black Hawk, slowly, ankles, and then wrists. He knelt before me with his head bowed. I unzipped the black hood that had bound him in darkness and released him to light and air.

Outside the door, the crowd began to applaud and whistle. I felt uneasy. A basic rule of scene play had been broken. The true name of a player had been revealed—*My name!* I could still feel my distress. But there wasn't much I really could do, so I ignored the situation and gathered up my equipment. Black Hawk had been so far removed by his endorphin state, I doubted that he had heard the commotion in the hallway. By the time we were ready to leave, the crowd had dispersed. I just wanted to go home and forget how uneasy it had made me feel.

One evening, a week later, I parked my car on the third level of the Union Street Garage across from Macy's downtown. The area where I parked was a good distance from the elevator, so with heightened awareness, I walked as quickly as possible towards it. As I approached, the door opened and a well-dressed businessman stepped out. As he walked toward me, I felt the intensity of his gaze. As he passed, I heard him say, "Excuse me! Don't I know you?"

"No, I don't think so," I said, and without hesitating, I continued toward the elevator, picking up my pace."

"Wait," he called after me. "I've seen you before. It's Diane, isn't it?" He knew my name! All I could think was that he must have seen me at Power Exchange! Was he a submissive looking for a dominant? Or, *does he think I am a prostitute?* The thought terrified me.

I quickly stepped inside the elevator and hoped he would not follow. Nothing about the moment felt safe, sane, or consensual. Blending into the crowd, I quickly finished my own shopping, unable to concentrate as I continued to contemplate what had happened. It wasn't a difficult decision that I made, right then and there—the night with Black Hawk would be the one and only time I ever performed scene play in public.

"You told Jack what had happened?" Tara asks, after I had finished retelling my story.

"No. As it turned out, I didn't need to say anything."

"What do you mean?" Tara asks.

"While I was still wondering how I was going to tell Jack about what happened, he mentioned that he wasn't interested in going to S&M play parties any more. 'I'm a submissive, and that's all I need to know,' he said."

"So, no more parties? No more out with his friends?" Tara asks. "All that effort *you* went through—to just stop?"

"Yep. No more parties. While he still participated in the volunteer group, to my knowledge he was no longer involved in the party scene. I was relieved."

"Considering everything you had gone through, I can imagine your sense of relief to get back to normal," Tara affirms.

I nod.

"Then imagine my surprise, a few weeks later, when Jack suggested we go to another Castle event. And, to top it off, he asked if I would go as his dominant? He said, it was a special event. At first, I balked, but he was adamant."

"And you relented and went? What happened?" Tara asks.

"I got more than I bargained for," I say, recalling the night.

Chapter 17

Clicking My Heels Together

I remember arriving at Jack's flat that evening. I pressed the intercom button and heard it buzz in the distant interior. As I waited, adrenalin coursed through my veins. The more I had thought about it, the more excited I had become about going to the 'Fem-Dom' party. While I was no longer interested in public exhibition, I saw this evening differently. It was a private party and I was acquainted with most of the people who would be attending. So, it allayed my concerns. I told myself that it could be fun and thought about what it might mean to Jack. When I said yes I would be willing to go, he had seemed happy, and added he wanted to try something different. He said he wanted to go in drag.

I was surprised because Jack had never shown an interest in dressing in drag. But, it was all about role-play, and when I thought more about it, I guessed Jack wanted to see how gender-funk would feel by wearing a dress in public. My only visual reference was the male subs I had once observed at another Fem-Dom party. One wore a dog collar and his female dominant led him around the party by a leash. Another man wore a dowdy housedress, poorly fitting support hose and

93

teetered on short, blocky 'old lady' heels that laced up the front. He wore a cheap, ill-fitting wig, which needed constant adjustment and his makeup was also poorly applied. Both men had followed their Dom doing her personal bidding and catering to her every whim. 'Dog-on-the-leash' had massaged her feet which were adorned in patterned black nylon. After which, she allowed him to thoroughly lick her bright red Dorothy of Oz-like shoes.

I found anyone willing to do this rather curious, but I was there to learn. While I could not say I understood what drove a person to do it, I tried to imagine the bigger picture. It was a member's only party, a place to express desires kept secret. If this was Jack's way of showing me his submissive nature, this was the place to do it. If having me lead him around on a leash was important to him, then so be it. I felt it must have some symbolic significance.

But I still was not sure what being a submissive meant to Jack. I understood it meant different things to different people, but Jack didn't fit the submissive role in my mind. I felt he must be working through feelings he had not fully shared. We hadn't attempted to play a scene together since The Castle, but with that experience under my belt, I saw this event as a sign that Jack wanted to explore his submissive side with me. So I felt that whatever came of the evening, I could dress the part. I was determined to overcome any misgivings, to surprise Jack, and to beef up my role. I dressed in the same costume I had worn at The Castle, but enhanced the look with the $289, thigh-high, four-inch stiletto boots!

I felt guilt at spending money I should use for household needs, but I decided I needed to go all out for this and I went even further, I cut my hair from shoulder-length to a chin-length bob, and dyed it blue-black. I used a black eyeliner, a dark mascara, and found a lipstick to match my nails called Midnight Red. As a last detail, I wore silver handcuff earrings I had purchased at the Folsom Street Fair.

Before heading for Jack's flat, I rechecked the toy bag for all the usual equipment, and added a leather dog collar I found at PetSmart, and its accompanying chain leash into the bag. I had not overlooked anything that I might need for the evening and the scene I had carefully constructed in my mind. I felt good knowing I would 'wow' Jack."

Chapter 18

Finding Myself in Oz

It took more time than I expected for Jack to release the door. As I pushed it open, I was surprised that the foyer light was off. The entry and stairwell were dark. I called out to Jack, but he didn't answer.

I remembered feeling butterflies of anticipation, but I had to get past my excitement and concentrate on ascending the dark stairwell. The stairs were steep and I didn't want to teeter off the stilettos. I left the toy bag at the bottom of the stairs, as I needed one hand on the stair rail and the other to lift my coat so I wouldn't trip over its hem. All the while, I anticipated reaching the top of the stairs where Jack, playing the part of a dowdy housewife, would greet me and begin the evening by asking to take my coat. When removed, it would reveal the sensual, sexy creature that lurked beneath—me!

I had gone up the stairs about halfway when Jack switched on the light. I reacted automatically and looked up. In that instant my life changed forever. An over whelming rush of emotion still accompanies the memory as the shock of that moment years before always hits me as fresh as if it happened yesterday.

On the landing above was Jack, poised with arms outstretched, like one commanding the stage and the audience's applause. But, it was not Jack! Instead stood a diva, dressed in a sleeveless, floor-length, black spandex gown that hugged every curve of his formulated womanly figure. His arms were adorned with elbow-length black spandex gloves. A thigh-high slit in his long dress showed a leg covered in sheer black nylon. Four-inch black patent stiletto heels peeked out from below its hem.

Shoulder-length, fine, auburn hair adorned his head. For a split second, Jack appeared uncertain, but quickly gathered confidence and a broad happy smile lit his features. He wore eye shadow of pale blue, perfectly lined eyes with dark liner, and eyelashes thickly coated with black mascara. The apples of his cheeks were delicately rouged, and his make-up was perfectly applied, right down to fully-lined rose-pink lips.

Jack did not wait for me to say anything. A soft, artificially feminine voice melodically said hello, as *she* batted *her* lashes in coy flirtation and asked, "Aren't I beautiful?"

I fought to control my surprise and tried to make sense of what I was seeing. In a flash, my world had turned upside down. What my eyes saw and what my mind was able to comprehend were two different things. I remember feeling an agonizing sense of confusion and with it, a sense of anxiety unlike anything I had ever experienced. A thousand questions raced through my mind.

I pulled my coat tight around me. My costume had become meaningless. Shame overcame the pride I had felt moments before. My efforts diminished and cheapened by the appearance and actions of the person I saw before me. What kept going through my mind was, *what does this mean?* I felt betrayed.

Chapter 19

The Sky Turned Green & The Grass Turned Blue

It was as if I had stepped into a Salvador Dali painting. My life's reality melted into surreal distortions. I hadn't just been surprised, I was in shock. My mind tried to wrap itself around what I was seeing, and simultaneously comprehend the meaning of it. My body was shaking, and I remember feeling I might vomit. I knew I would faint if I didn't sit down. I don't remember climbing the remaining stairs, reaching the top landing, walking into the adjacent hallway, or leaning against the wall, before I slipped down and sat on the floor. I remember struggling for air, and I heard Jack's angry voice telling me to take deep breaths. As the pounding in my head cleared, questions formed with lightning speed.

"What does this mean?" I gasped, barely able to find my voice. I had thought to myself, *no woman puts make-up on that perfectly the first time!* My mind understood. Her attire had been perfect. Not just in a dress, but in elegance. Not as a humble matron, but as a queen. Then it hit me. Jack hadn't intended to go to the party as a submissive to show me homage, but rather, to be the one in the spotlight.

Then, I heard his voice screaming at me. He was angry. "Fuck you! Fuck you! I hate you!"

He's angry? Why is HE angry? I thought, my mind swirling. But no doubt, my face reflected my shock and confusion.

His voice broke, and I remember thinking, *is he going to cry?* I didn't know what to make of it. Then, he kicked the high heels off of his feet, and tore at the elbow-length gloves on his arms, throwing the gloves against the wall. He began to pace angrily back and forth, up and down the hall.

I screamed, "talk to me!" as he tore off the wig and threw it on the floor. It didn't matter to me if he wore the clothes. I only wanted to understand the agenda. Furthering my confusion, I sensed more than anger in his voice—there was genuine hurt.

My mind was in such a muddle, I didn't know what to make of it. So I just sat on the floor, trying to get a grip. Moments later, I realized Jack had removed the dress and was standing over me stripped down to only sheer black panty hose, and a black fabric corset with a padded bra that helped contour his own lanky frame into a woman's shape. He glared at me in angry pouting silence from a face covered in make-up that now seemed almost clown-like. The skullcap that controlled his sparse hair under the auburn wig sat at an angle on his head. The moment would have been laughable—if it wasn't real.

"Jack, this isn't something you just *do*," I said, looking up at him and speaking in a voice as controlled and calm as I could muster. "I want answers, not a fight."

He yelled, "Fuck you, Diane, Fuck you."

I didn't know how to respond, but his words hurt." His demeanor changed as he picked up the black patent heels, and silently slipped them back onto his feet. I was trying to hold onto reason and control my emotion; but I felt I had lost him. I felt helpless. Then, I got angry.

"Tell me what this means?" I said, my voice beginning to rise.

"You won't understand this, Diane," he shouted back.

"Try me!" I screamed. "What I understand right now is that you owe me an explanation! It looks like you've been lying to me Jack, about a lot of things!"

"I haven't lied to you. At least, I didn't *mean* to lie to you!" he said angrily.

Jack began to retreat down the hallway, the stilettos clicking loudly on the hardwood floor. As he went, he picked up pieces of clothing, and then disappeared into the back of the Victorian.

I picked myself up off of the floor. I wanted to leave, but not without answers. I followed Jack down the hall, pausing only to pick up one of the black gloves that he had missed. Jack had gone into the kitchen.

I found him standing in front of the mirrored accent wall that bordered the breakfast nook. Calm and self-absorbed, as if in a trance, he was admiring his image in the mirror. The black evening gown was draped over a bar stool. Jack had readjusted the nylon skullcap and replaced the wig. One-by-one, he tweaked at the curls with his fingers so that they would be in perfect place. He pursed his lips as he reached for a tube of lipstick that lay on the counter, all the while captivated, never taking his eyes off the vision that peered back at him. I watched as he applied with perfect precision more rose-colored gloss. Blotting his lips together to assure an even application, he gazed up and down at his reflection, giving it an approving smile.

He had to have known I was watching. Standing behind him, I was reflected in the mirror, but it was as though I didn't exist. I continued to watch dumfounded. He struck a seductive pose on the back of one of the bar stools, his eyes never straying from the mirror. He tossed his head back and shook the auburn hair away from his face, admiring the contour of his chest bound in the corset, and the appearance of a swelling bosom within the push-up bra. He then uttered, "I am desirable."

Caught up in the moment, I thought to myself with some fascination, that he really *could* pass for a female. The person reflected in the mirror was stunning. To anyone else, seeing him at the top of the stairs, and not knowing, he would have been a beautiful woman. I tried to get my mind around it. Nothing about what I was witnessing felt real. It took some moments before I made myself ask, "You've dressed like this before?"

His eyes did not leave his own reflection, but he laughed lightly and the artificially feminine voice said, "Yes, many times."

Who are you? I thought at that moment. *Not Jack! Whoever you are, you are not Jack!*

"Have you gone out in public like this?" I pursued, afraid of his answer. "Have people seen you dressed like this?"

He laughed as if the joke was on me. "Of course," he said, lowering his gaze demurely, as he turned to look at me. "At private events."

His laugh felt cruel, and by his attitude, I could see no empathy for what I was feeling. I wanted to hear that this was the only time he had done this. I wanted an explanation that was something I could deal with.

I fired questions at him. "Are you gay? Did you lie to me back when we had our HIV tests? You said you weren't interested in men."

"I didn't lie to you, Diane, I've told you before, I'm *not* gay!" he said.

102

"But you've been with men, Jack. What am I supposed to think? What am I to you?" I shouted, bombarding him with questions.

He wouldn't answer. He just paced the room silently.

I didn't know what to think, so I just continued to barrage him with questions.

"Where did you get the clothes?" I asked. He didn't hesitate, saying, he wore a size eleven in women's shoes. "I found these on the internet, but I have gotten others through catalogues," he offered.

Others? My anxiety was growing. He took the black floor-length dress from the bar stool, held it up to himself and said, "Don't you think this dress is wonderful? I think it fits my figure so well! I found it at Foxy Lady. It's a great shop in the Mission. The shop girl let me try it on before I purchased it so that I knew it would fit. She said it looked great on me. So, I bought it! She was right, don't you think? It hugs every curve!"

"What about the wig and the makeup?" I asked, not letting up.

"The wig—this old thing?" he said, as he looked admiringly at the auburn hairpiece that crowned his head and brushed at his shoulders when he moved.

It's not new, was the information I quickly absorbed.

"Helen—she's so helpful! We decided that this color was perfect for my skin tone. I think she was right, don't you?" he asked, as he moved closer to the mirror to examine his makeup with a critical eye.

"Your makeup . . . the blue eye shadow matches your eyes. How did you get the liner on so perfectly?" I asked. I thought he must have had help. I knew the make-up that I kept in the drawer in the guest bathroom for when I stayed over did not match with anything he was wearing. For a fleeting instant, I wondered if there was another woman.

Jack turned from the mirror, placed the dress back on the bar stool, and walked toward me, reaching out for my hand. He led me out of the kitchen towards the master bedroom. He said, "Wait here," and left me standing in the doorway near the foot of the queen-sized bed. He walked over to the closet, opened the door and went inside. Rummaging around on an overhead shelf, he pulled down a shoebox. He returned, stopping in front of me, eyes downcast, and submissively extended the box. When he did look up, it was with a sad, but compliant stare.

"Here," he said. "You wanted to know. Take it."

I took the box and walked to the bed and sat down. It was a regular gray cardboard shoebox that had seen some use. The corners of the lid were worn. I noticed that it had once held women's shoes, size eleven. Carefully, I removed the lid.

It was full of cosmetics: eye shadow of almost every hue, multiple tubes of lipstick and gloss, mascara in black, brown, blue, and liners to match. There were compacts of pressed powder, some liquid make-up, various blushes, rouge, make-up brushes, eye and other make-up remover. It appeared that all of the items had been used many times.

"These are mine," he said, as he dared to sit down on the bed next to me.

I looked at him in disbelief because it was way too much for my mind to absorb. In the seven years I had known him, in the normal occurrence of staying over on weekends, and opening cupboards, drawers, closets, I had never run across any of the items he was showing me.

As I looked in the box, I remembered a time not long after we had been dating, when I opened a bathroom drawer looking for a mirror and found a tube of red lipstick. *Was he seeing someone else?* I had wondered at the time. When I asked him, he said it belonged to his ex-wife, and that she had left it when she had visited a couple of weeks before. He had just thrown it in the drawer. I knew she had visited, so I didn't question it. Now I wondered how I could have been so blind.

"I have never seen this make-up, Jack," I said to him.

"You've never seen these things in my home because I hide them or I purge!" Jack said.

"Purge?" I questioned. "What do you mean by that?"

"Throw them out! I find a dumpster or a trash can on the street and throw everything away. There was a time I would buy clothes and make-up and go out on the town. Now I just wear them at home. When I met you, I became afraid someone would recognize me when I went out or, that you might find out. I try not to keep anything, except make-up. That's easy to hide."

"How long have you been doing this?" I asked.

"Since my late teens," he said. He reminded me again of trips he would take to New York as a teen. He had always loved the museums.

"I would do it then. You can be anonymous in New York, and now, when I go on vacation."

"Is that why you never want me to go on trips with you Jack?" I asked. He nodded.

"When I travel, I entertain myself by shopping for clothes and make-up and I dress in my room. Sometimes I want to go out, but I don't have the nerve to go out in cities I'm not familiar with." He shuddered and I saw a flicker of fear cross his face.

"In D.C, and Seattle," I asked, "did you dress there also?"

"Yes. At the end of the trip I get rid of everything, usually in an airport restroom. I throw everything away before I board the plane home. Remember, in Seattle when I called you, freaking out because my rental car had been broken into?"

"They stole your luggage,' I said, remembering his panicked phone call, his terrified voice.

"I thought, perhaps someone from the convention saw me, and got back at me by breaking into my car, stealing my clothes, my makeup—everything," he affirmed. "For weeks afterward, I worried that someone from the conference would contact me—out me." I could see by his expression that he was still afraid.

"But still, you dress like this here . . . in the city?" I pursued undeterred, wanting to know.

"Yes," he admitted.

"Where do you go? Do you go out in public? Private parties? Does the community know? Am I the only one who *doesn't* know?" I thought of his new friends and my fear was turning to anger. *What else was he hiding?*

"One question at a time, Diane," said Jack in a condescending tone. Had my questions caught up with him?

"Yes, I go out in public," he exclaimed. "I try to pick and choose where I go though, and, *who* I go with."

He hadn't been going with me! That much I knew.

Suddenly, I recalled another member of the community pulling me aside after a class to ask if Jack dressed in drag because he thought he had seen him with a group of people on Polk Street one night a few weeks before. With no thought that it could have been him, I had said no. *Jack doesn't dress in drag.* Now I wondered, *what if it was him, and what if he was recognized by someone outside of the BDSM community—one of his patients?* Realizations were bringing new fears. It could mean the end of his career."

106

Before I could say anything else, Jack let the cat out of the bag. He said, "One of the docs I know saw me one night when I was out. Later that week he stopped me in the hall at the hospital and asked me out." Jack's laugh was soft, and his cheeks turned rosy pink at the memory.

"Did you go out with him?" I asked Jack.

Jack smiled. "Yes. Actually, I did, a few weeks later."

Jack said that a part of him wanted to see where it would go. He said that all it took was having dinner with him to re-affirm that he wasn't interested in men.

"We've talked about this before, Diane, I am *not* gay. My preference is women. I don't even like men. They scare me. I could never have a relationship with a man."

But he had not convinced me. Rather, he had given me reason to doubt everything he had ever said to me. I was feeling flooded by a sense of betrayal by the man I loved and thought loved me!

Jack removed the wig and set it on an androgynous Styrofoam head he took from the closet and placed on the dresser. "Which doc was it?" I asked.

I knew all of them through my work. My curiosity wanted an answer as to which one had wanted a man in drag, and who was this person that Jack had been attracted enough to, that he would consider going out to dinner with him.

"Jack started to laugh, a deeper and less pretentious laugh, then his answer cut deep, further undermining any trust I had. "You will remember him, Diane. Two years ago, at the Castro Street Fair when we bumped into the two docs. You got mad at me because I introduced you as my friend and not as my girlfriend or significant other? Later I told you he thought you were my sister."

"Yes, I remember," I said, recalling two years earlier how he had introduced me. We had argued about it later, his lack of acknowledgement of me as his girlfriend—*more than just an oversight*, I had felt. I remembered how it troubled me. Jack had said he was sorry, but now I felt they had been just words.

At that point, Jack said, "I am tired, Diane, can we stop this discussion?" It was clear he would talk no more.

I was stunned. I just sat there. It felt so unreal. I watched, dumbfounded, as Jack removed the corset, stopping to show me the special gel inserts in the bra, and chatting about how he had purchased them to help feminize his form. Then he removed the shear black nylons and a pair of woman's purple, silk bikini panties. He turned to me smiling as he pointed to his crotch. Artfully, his penis and scrotum had been bound by surgical tape, pulled back and up against the pelvis so as not to protrude. A technique he explained that was used to disguise maleness.

Once the tape was removed, which did not seem to cause him any discomfort at all, he reached for a white dress shirt he had hung haphazardly across the bedroom chair and put it on. He walked barefoot towards the bathroom, skull cap still in place, and make-up still in its state of perfection.

I was overwhelmed by what had happened and by what he said. I had some answers, but not the ones I needed. And I didn't know how to handle the feelings I was experiencing: anxiety, confusion, and dread, I was afraid—scared about what I didn't know. It was like the bogeyman was still under the bed. I was still anticipating the unknown. I remember I just sat there on the bed feeling numb and trying to piece it all together. He hadn't come back when I finally stood up.

I glanced down at myself. The long black coat was still buttoned up.

The entire time I was there, I had never taken my coat off and Jack had never seen my outfit.

I walked out of the bedroom, and still not seeing Jack anywhere, I walked as quickly as I could, down the steep stairs without tripping. I picked up the toy bag. I let myself out of the flat. I did not say goodbye to Jack. I did not feel that he would even know or care that I had left. I clutched my coat tight about me and hoped that the cocoon of support it gave might help keep me steady until I could reach my car. I was weak-kneed, shaking, and the knot in my stomach hadn't let up. I moved fast across the dark street toward my car, forcing back a need to scream. My mind was still in chaos, not knowing what was happening. *What's next?* I climbed in and started my car, pulled out and headed toward Divisadero Street. By the time, I reached Washington, I was in full-blown panic mode with feelings I couldn't sort through and questions without answers. Our relationship—my life—had taken a bizarre turn.

Unable to drive, I pulled over on the outskirts of nowhere and just sat in the car, crying and screaming.

* * *

Tara had sat silent, listening, as I let it all out, seeming to have understood my need to vent.

"Unbelievable, Diane, just unbelievable. I don't know what to say. I can't imagine what I would have done in your place." The look of surprise and distress on her face said it all. She was clearly shaken.

But before we could talk further, and as if it were pre-ordained, Tara's cell phone went off. It was Len.

"Shit! Please, not now, Len!" Tara exclaims as she listens to her messages. "Crap! He's asked me to bring him the contract!" She hesitates as if debating whether to go or not. "Diane, I can be back in forty-five minutes or less. Please, will you wait for me? I don't want to go. I want to hear the rest of this."

"Sure, I will just sit here and stroll down Memory Lane," I smile. Truth be told, I knew I would welcome the chance to regroup my thoughts.

"Tell me this much before I go," Tara asks. "You decided it was over, right?"

"The end? It was just the beginning."

Chapter 20

Smoke and Mirrors

After Tara left, I ordered a Coke and continued to reminisce about what had come next after Jack's big reveal. The next morning, I awoke to a ringing telephone, surprised to find it was Jack wanting to talk. When I had seen him the night before, with the skillfully applied makeup and in the fashionable evening gown, my gut told me that this was more than a charade and the realization had left me an emotional mess. A myriad of questions swirled in my head, but they all boiled down to one, *What does it all mean?* So even my mounting trepidation did not hold me back. I agreed to meet because we needed to talk.

When I arrived at the condo, Jack rang me in. On ascending the stairs, I quickly discovered, it wasn't the Jack I expected to see. He was sitting on the living room sofa, listening to Depeche Mode's *Walking in My Shoes*, dressed in ladies tailored black slacks and a soft pink sweater. His blue eyes were accentuated by freshly applied liner, and his cheeks were tinted with a sweater-matching pink blush. The auburn tresses of the night before had been replaced. Now a contemptuous glare struck out at me through swooping bangs of strawberry-blond hair that gracefully brushed his shoulders. In a gesture of feminine defiance, the Jack I did not know tossed his head, swinging his stylish mane.

I just stood and stared, swallowed hard, and took in what I saw. My confusion was undoubtedly written all over my face. This wasn't what I had been expecting. I was expecting an apology.

"You should have known, Diane!" said the pastel-pink lips curled into an irritated scowl. Jack had rebuked me before I had uttered a single word.

He stood and slipped on the same black patent heels I remembered from the evening before, and then defiantly click-clacked his way past me, down the long hallway of the Victorian. As the sound of the heels kicked at my psyche, I followed, speechless, past the rose-pink guest bathroom, the daffodil-colored bedroom, and into the Martha Stewart kitchen with the black-and-white checkerboard floor, stainless steel appliances, and the wall of spotless mirror.

"Known, Jack? Explain to me how I was supposed to have guessed your secret?" I asked, rising to my own defense.

"Think about it! The clues were all around you!" He grandly gestured at the surroundings that I knew did not reflect the taste of the average male. *Had I been naïve to believe that when Jack had asked and taken my suggestions about decorating the flat that he might be preparing a home we might both enjoy?*

"From how you decorate your apartment I was supposed to have guessed that you're a cross-dresser?" I asked.

As he turned, I thought I caught the faint glimmer of a cat-that-swallowed-the-canary smile, but yet his voice was tinged with vexation. "You really don't get it, do you Diane? There were times I thought you might guess," he laughed as if the joke had been on me.

"The apartment on Baker . . . remember the lipstick you found in the drawer?"

"It wasn't your ex's?"

"No, it was mine," he confirmed. "And the room I asked you not to go into because I used it for storage . . ."

I remembered the open window on the third floor and a beige curtain whipping in the wind. *That room? Jack's apartment window!* "I remember," I said.

"It was my dressing room. I had a couple of full-length mirrors in there, and that was where I kept my clothes and my make-up."

Jack's look was matter-of-fact. I took it to mean that he was relieved that the truth was out.

"I had no reason not to trust you, Jack," I countered. "Now you're saying I should have known by what you kept hidden from me that you're a cross-dresser?"

Jack's eyes burned with renewed exasperation. "A cross-dresser! No, Diane! *Not* a cross-dresser. I don't just want to wear women's clothes. I want to *be* a woman!"

I choked, as my mind spun a 360. *Who does this?* I thought. Then memory served me up with a vision of an unusually tall working girl standing at a corner on Polk Street. A he/she, someone had said. Now, faced with Jack's admission, wheels had been set in motion. My mind raced to review the past and search for the clues I must have missed.

Chapter 21

Hormones or Psychosis

"You say, I should have known, Jack! But, you went out of your way to hide things from me." Recalling his betrayal, I could hardly control my outrage. "Among other things, you said, 'I purge!' As often as I am at your apartment, it must have been a challenge to constantly hide things from me." I envisioned him scrambling through the flat in a panic searching for items he may not have hidden as I pushed his doorbell.

The defiant look on Jack's face had mellowed. Perhaps, because he knew I was right.

"Anything else to confess? What else have you kept from me, Jack? Now's the time, spit it out!" I harangued him with my anger.

"All right, Diane . . . all right!" Jack paced the floor, his anger turning to compliance. "Hormones, I've been taking hormones." He stopped pacing and looked directly at me, waiting for the fallout.

"Hormones! What do you mean, hormones?"

"Hormones, HRT—hormone replacement— estrogen. I've been taking what I need to take to make changes. To change me from this . . ." he swept his hands dramatically down his sides, and across his torso in encompassing circles, "to . . . I want to be a *woman*,

115

Diane!" His eyes were filled with frustration and his expression held an underlying sadness.

"You're telling me that you have been taking hormones . . . to . . ."

"To become who I want to be in *here!*" Jack interrupted, pressing his hand against his heart.

"How long, Jack?" I asked, not believing what I was hearing.

"Off and on over the last three years, Diane." He looked at the floor like a child caught with his hand in the cookie jar.

"I'll take them for a few weeks, then go off them. I would get scared that you, or others, would notice changes."

"What kind of changes, Jack?" I asked, wondering if I might have seen, but missed something.

"My skin—softer; breast development—swelling; emotions—a woman's emotions."

The world of my mind wobbled on its axis while its sky turned green and its grass turned blue. His words, "I want to be a woman," "changes," "hormones," swirled inside my head, morphing my vision of Jack. *Jack wants to be a she?* I struggled to think. *You need to focus!* My inner-self said. I began to remember other things I hadn't been able to explain, like the evening a year before after we had dinner at Star India on Geary Boulevard.

* * *

We had walked back to Jack's car, which was parked on Arguello near Clement Street. Not only had it seemed like a very long work week, but it had also been the week when Jack's convertible's soft-top had been slashed in the dead of night, while parked in front of his affluent Pacific Heights home. Jack had shrugged it off, but it left me feeling on edge. I could never understand why someone would do that.

116

With the incident still in the forefront of my mind, I couldn't help but be cautiously alert to our surroundings as we walked down the dark street dotted with dying street lamps. And, while he denied it, Jack was obviously stressed out by the week's traumas as he continued to ruminate about what had happened in animated fashion. Upon reaching the car, he stopped talking and suddenly turned away from me, walking into the dark shadows of a nearby building.

"Jack?" I called out as he moved away. I heard him laugh and saw him shake his head. *What had I said?* I wondered. He spoke a few sentences I couldn't hear, before blurting out "Fuck you!" It was then I realized he wasn't talking to me. *Was there someone, lurking in the shadows?* I stayed at the curb, anxiously waiting for his return.

"Jack, what's going on?" I called, as he moved back toward me. "Who were you talking to?"

He looked at me with unseeing eyes, before turning away again and responding to a voice only he could hear.

"Jack!" I called out. Now I realized there had been no one in the shadows.

"Jack! I'm right here. What are you doing?" As he turned back towards me, he smiled at me as if nothing had happened.

"I want to go to Green Apple Books, Diane," he said matter-of-factly and without explanation. He picked up his pace in the direction of the store, "You think they're still open?"

"What?" I asked, following along and trying to remain calm as I tried to sort through what I had just seen and heard. On alert, I continued to watch Jack and wonder if I had misinterpreted something. We rounded the corner onto Clement and spotted the bookstore a couple of blocks away.

Green Apple Books' bright lights and aura of general calm seemed to quiet things. Jack's normal routine of beginning in the calendar section renewed my sense of order.

"Look Jack, here's that Gothic Art calendar you looked for at Borders. They were out of it, remember?" I imagined his excitement at finding it, but instead, Jack suddenly shoved past me and headed for the second floor.

"Jack! Wait a minute," I called after him.

"You stay down here!" he commanded. "I'll be back in five minutes."

Left in his wake, my unsettled feeling returned.

"I'll be in the art section," I replied weakly. Usually Jack let me tag along. *What's up with him*, I wondered unhappily.

Five minutes turned into fifteen and fifteen into a half hour, but still no Jack. Concerned, I went to the second floor and began to check the stacks and hidden alcoves, growing more concerned with each unsuccessful pass.

Could he have left without me noticing? Not likely, my inner voice reassured me.

A quick search of the first floor revealed no Jack. On the second floor, I looked into the history room, and walked a narrow catwalk, which led to a larger room full of paperbacks and the store's office. Finally, I spotted Jack sitting cross-legged on the floor in a small tight corner of the metaphysical section. His back was towards me and his arms were wrapped tight about his torso. He rocked back and forth, chanting what sounded like a mantra in a low but menacing tone.

"Jack?" I whispered. He did not change his position or acknowledge me.

"Jack," I repeated louder this time, my frustration building. "I've been worried. You didn't come back and

118

I've been waiting for you almost an hour. Are you ready to go?"

Jack turned. His facial expression was contorted into a twisted sneer reflecting rage and hate. *What did I do?* I asked myself, as he spit and hissed unintelligible words and rose from his position, unwinding his body in snake-like fashion.

Nothing, you've done nothing! My inner voice answered. But I stepped back.

Standing, Jack remained slightly hunched, as if he would strike.

"Why can't you leave me alone? I don't want you here! I told you I had something to do. You were supposed to wait!"

Grabbing my arm in a vice-like grip, he continued to snarl within inches of my face.

"Jack, let go!" I said, recoiling from his grip. I staggered back against a bookcase, my eyes never leaving his. *What's gotten into him?* I thought. *He's never acted this way before!*

In what seemed to be a split second, his demeanor changed.

"Oh, here you are!" he smiled, merging back into my reality, "Are you done looking around? I couldn't find the book I was looking for. You ready to go?" He asked, heading for the stairs, without waiting for an answer.

What had just happened? I found myself shaken and confused. I watched Jack head down the stairwell, stopping to pick up the Gothic Art calendar. He spoke to the sales clerk, joking and laughing. Now he was the Jack I had known for six years. I watched closely—and it was the same old Jack, the Jack I thought I knew.

I was reluctant to leave the store with him. I didn't know what to think.

"Jack, before we go, let me show you what I found," I insisted, pulling him back into the art section to show him a first edition Cameo book on Persian rugs. I offered him a piece of candy I had bought while I was waiting. All the while, I was looking for further reassurance of his usual normal behavior. My mind still reeling, I continued to repeat the question, *what just happened?* I knew I had not imagined it.

"Did the Indian food agree with you, Jack?" I asked.

"The food was great! I feel great!" Jack smiled.

"So, you didn't find the book you were looking for?" I probed.

"They don't have it, but there's a store on Telegraph in Berkeley that should."

"What is the title?" I pursued.

"It's a wiccan book, *Women and Witchcraft*," Jack answered.

"Are you walking along the edge of the abyss again Jack? Devils and witches?"

I recalled a conversation in which Jack had referenced hanging onto the edge of an abyss most of his life, and that he had always feared falling into it. I thought, *maybe if I can get him to talk, we can discuss the strange events of this evening, because he seemed totally unaware of what had happened.*

"It's just a book, Diane," Jack replied without energy. "You want this?" He pulled the Cameo first edition from the shelf where I had replaced it. "Here, I'll get it for you. It will be a nice addition to your art book collection. I'm sorry I took so long," he apologized suddenly.

He's trying to make everything okay, I thought, clutching the book as we rode back to Jack's flat. Still disturbed by Jack's unusual behavior, I wondered about my decision to stay over as I usually did on Saturday nights. The kids *did* have a sitter.

"I'm looking forward to going to the Palace of Fine Arts tomorrow," Jack said, as we arrived at his condo.

"Me, too," I said.

"I'm going to get a glass of water, Diane. Do you want one?" Jack asked, after we had ascended the stairs. He haphazardly threw his jacket over the stairwell banister and headed for the kitchen.

"No thank you," I replied, my voice trailed after him as I headed to the bedroom. *Maybe sleep will help*, I thought. I stripped away my blouse, blue jeans and underwear, and tossed them onto a chair in the corner of the room. Slipping naked between the salmon pink Egyptian cotton sheets, noting their cool softness against my skin, I pulled the floral print comforter up under my chin, relaxed, and let my mind drift.

"No!" Jack's voice shouted angrily. "No! No! NO!"

Believing he was talking on his cell phone, I wondered, *what would possess a patient to call so late? Jack hated to be interrupted after office hours. It was 10:30 p.m.!* I watched as Jack stormed past the open bedroom door. He was barefoot and wore only a T-shirt.

"Jack?" I called out as he walked by again, his hands on his hips.

His voice continued its angry rant. Hands on hips? I realized he wasn't on his cell phone. So *who was he talking to?* He passed the door again, seemingly unaware of my presence. *Had some other person invaded his psyche?* Jack continued to walk up and down the hall, working himself into a frenzy. I flattened myself against the mattress and pulled the comforter up around me. Hidden from view, I peered over the top. The light from the small brass hallway lamp revealed Jack's red face contorted in anger. His arms were crossed tight against his chest and rope-like veins coursed his neck as he hissed words of bitterness and contempt towards his partner in conversation.

"All you women, you're all the same!" he snarled in a voice rising with agitation.

I lay silent in the darkness with my eyes wide open.

"I hate you! Leave me alone! Get away from me!" He picked up a book that lay near the lamp and flung it against the stairwell wall. I heard it tumble down the steep flight of stairs and began to shiver as I listened to his menacing rant. I hoped that Jack would not remember that I was there.

As he passed the open bedroom door one last time before going down the hall to the bathroom, I heard the sound of a clenched fist strike a wall. Then the bathroom door slammed shut.

I threw back the bed covers. There was no time to dress. I pulled a long beige raincoat from Jack's closet, and threw it on, and quickly grabbed my clothes and shoes, stuffing them into my shoulder bag. With the bag tight against my chest, I struggled to keep the large coat wrapped closed about my naked frame. I quickly and quietly descended the stairs, pushed the door open and still barefoot, fled to the safety and darkness of the street.

I was terrified by the mysterious behavior I could neither understand or explain. Jack would never admit remembering what happened that night. And while it never happened again, I worried that it was some form of psychosis. But now, armed with Jack's newest disclosure, I wondered, was it hormones?

Chapter 22

Unraveling the Mystery

When Jack finally came out to me, we had been together a little over seven years. As I thought back over that time, initially, I couldn't recall having seen any evidence of his secret. But the more I thought about it, the more I realized Jack had been right. The clues had been all around. That tube of lipstick was just the first clue. But I wanted to know, *what else had I missed?*

In the fall of 1992, Jack moved from the Baker Street apartment to his condo in Pacific Heights. I sat on the patterned circle of Persian carpet on the hand-waxed hardwood floor of Jack's flat on a lazy Sunday afternoon, admiring the dark wood bookcases that stretched up to the ten-foot ceiling. Jack had turned the alcove next to the living room into a small library. In this quiet, meditative place, the sun was quietly sinking over the western horizon as we opened the last of the boxes that had come from his family home the week before. Upon his father's death and sale of the house, what had remained of Jack's childhood had been placed in several cardboard boxes by his only brother before being shipped to Jack in San Francisco. That afternoon we were putting them away. I remembered grabbing a book from one of the small piles that lay scattered on the floor and scrambling to my feet to lift the *World Atlas* towards the geography shelf.

It had been a day of reflection as we went through the boxes and explored remnants of Jack's past. As he sorted the contents, he reminisced with stories of his childhood. Jack reached for a Victorian table lamp and twisted the small brass knob at its base. When the light came on, it did little to brighten the darkening space.

"That didn't help much, did it?" Jack saw as he opened a large scrapbook of college pictures he had on his lap. It was obvious he did not want to get up from where he sat cross-legged to flip the wall switch for the much-needed overhead light.

"I'll get it, Jack," I offered. It was a much-needed opportunity to stretch the kinks from my legs. Taking inventory of the remaining stacks of paperbacks, I picked a copy of Walt Whitman's *Leaves of Grass* from the box and managed to squeeze it in next to Ralph Waldo Emerson's *Quatrains* beside other poetry books on the fourth shelf.

"We're almost done, but we may run out of space," I said, pointing out that most of the shelves were nearly full.

Jack had not heard me. He was focused intently on the scrapbook. I recognized it as the same one he had replaced on the top shelf earlier in the afternoon after it toppled off its perch. The scrapbook had fallen, crashing to the floor as Jack had been atop a stepstool trying to squeeze another book, into an already full shelf. As the scrapbook splayed open, a piece of notebook paper slipped out and pirouetted onto the polished oak floor. Attempting to help, I bent to retrieve it when the phrase *flower of the mountain* printed neatly on faded blue lines jumped out at me.

"Here, I'll take that!" Jack said, stepping down quickly to take it from my hand. Without another word, he folded it and secreted the piece under a photo in the scrapbook before again placing it onto a shelf high overhead.

Flower of the Mountain. I recalled that it was the piece that Jack had read to me in City Lights. *The passage must have more meaning to Jack than I know*, I thought then but did not say. Now, I wondered. *Was the piece by James Joyce a reflection of Jack's own passionate feminine desire?*

Turning quickly through its worn pages, Jack stopped flipping pages only to sip through a bent straw that protruded from a can of Diet Pepsi. He always asked for a straw. I recalled how a male friend had once said, "Real men don't use straws." *Was this another clue?*

"Looking at these pictures, I am reminded . . ." Jack's voice trailed off as he thumbed through the fragile pages of his past. "This was the summer I ate nothing but hamburgers!" He laughed, pointing at a photo of himself with friends at a summer picnic.

"Why do you *DO* that Jack?" I had asked. Since I had known him, he had often gone on food binges. For a week at a time, he would eat only a muffin and drink several cups of Martha & Bros. coffee each day. Other times, he skipped breakfast altogether, drank Diet Pepsi all day, and ate only a single Barber Stuffed Chicken Cordon Bleu for dinner.

"Do what?" he asked, inadvertently adjusting his black-rimmed glasses, not looking up; he was still intent on the photos.

"Drink only Diet Pepsi and eat muffins!" I laughed.

When he looked up, he was stern, serious, and answered without a hint of levity. "I want to stay thin."

It's usually women who talk about wanting to be thin, I thought. *Is being thin his vision of himself as a woman?*

"But it's not healthy, Jack!" I said. "A strong wind could blow you over."

Before I could engage him further in conversation, he interjected, "Oh look! Those were good times!"—"There's Pete!" He held the scrapbook up to the light and urged me to look.

"Pete? Is that your friend from high school?" I had heard Jack speak of their juvenile antics. "Where's he now?" I asked.

"I'm not sure. Last I saw him was in Boston the year I graduated from college."

Jack handed me a loose photo that had slipped untethered from its corner anchors.

"That was the summer I fell in love!" he exclaimed, as he unfolded the small sheet of blue-lined notebook paper that earlier had been shoved beneath the photo. He smiled as he read it to himself. *The passage does have special meaning to Jack*, I thought.

I re-examined the photo he had handed me of two girls and three college boys lounging on a campus lawn, one of whom was Jack. The girls were sunbathing on a blanket as the boys sat around a picnic table, eating hamburgers. "Which one is she?" I asked. The boys appeared to be in an intent conversation. Schoolbooks were scattered on the grass.

My question had been left unanswered, as Jack rummaged through another box of books, intent on finding one in particular. Now I wondered, *was it possible Jack's summer of love hadn't been a girl, but a boy?*

"There's a book that should be in here, but I don't see it," he frowned. "I hope it's in the other box."

Annoyed with not finding it, he picked up a remaining small tower of paperbacks that sat on the floor and threw them back into the box.

"Have you ever read *Conundrum*?" he asked, suddenly.

I immediately visualized a small, well-read book in my mother's library. That he and I had read the same book of challenging psychological puzzles brought a smile to my face. *Something else we have in common! I had thought, it's the little things that bring people together.* We often spoke of our mutual interest in books. He was a collector of history, poetry, geography and humor, while I favored small out-of-print books, children's stories and art.

"I did," I answered. "I found it thought-provoking. I read it several times."

"You did?" Jack looked surprised, and then smiled. "The first time I read it, I was fourteen. Well, it doesn't seem to be here. Since it's out-of-print, I don't expect I will ever find it easily again. Perhaps we can put it on our 'look for list' when we go to the Antiquarian Book Faire?"

I thought to myself, that if I could find *Little Sallie Mandy*, another childhood book, I could find *Conundrum*, a book of puzzles. *Jack's a puzzle*, I thought.

As my mind continued to search through the past seven years I had spent with Jack, seeking the details I had missed that would make the big picture clear, I remembered Jack's car. *The sport convertible's soft-top had been vandalized five times. Jack refused to report the incidents to the police. Now it made sense. It had to be someone who knew Jack was dressing as a female, most likely a neighbor. A hater, I thought, now worried that Jack could be putting his life at risk. He must have suspected, but how would I have known? What else had I missed?*

"I'm a submissive, and that's all I need to know," he insisted.

In fact, was Jack's involvement in the S&M community not a man's interest in s-e-x, or, exploring his male submissive side, but rather, a means to research his gender and his own personal sexual identity? Was the meaning of "I'm a submissive," actually a statement about being a woman at heart and his belief that women are submissive? Was his involvement in the S&M community, where diversity and experimentation within boundaries is an accepted norm, *only* about having a safe place to act out the role of a woman safely, and to test what it would be like to be a female through role-play, and to dress the part? There he could experiment with his feminine side and no one would question him. *But how could I have known?*

As I tried to sort out the clues dropped like bread crumbs along the forest floor over years, the shoulda, woulda, coulda of guessing his secret might have happened if all of the pieces of this human puzzle had been together at one time to view. But, that hadn't been the case. The pieces of this puzzle had been scattered over time. Now I was faced with another dilemma: *Do I stay or do I go?*

Chapter 23

Mind Maze

My appointment was for two o'clock. Finding parking on Webster had proved an unexpected challenge. Not wanting to be late, I ran to the corner crosswalk, only to watch the bumper-to-bumper traffic on California Street inch forward through the intersection as I waited for the light to change. Once across the intersection, I strained my eyes to read the numbers on the old homes. I reread my hand-scribbled note and confirmed that the once stately Victorian before me was indeed the correct address. A home faded by time, its steep, well-worn wooden steps, flanked by pots of small colorful flowers, creaked as I climbed.

It had been nearly three weeks since I made the appointment. It had been an agonizing wait. I needed answers and had been forming questions I might ask. It had always bothered me that Jack hadn't been able to remember the strange episode he had experienced, but now, armed with his coming out and his use of hormones, I had tried to put two and two together. I still wondered if it was hormones or psychosis. *That* question was one of many I had for the psychologist.

My mind was still a maze of unanswered questions and I kept running into walls. I felt I was in a mind warp. I didn't know if up was down, or down was up.

"Don't leave me, Diane! I don't want you to leave me," Jack had pleaded when I voiced my concerns. When he asked for reassurance, all I could say was, "I don't know what I'm going to do." Then he had said, "I'm seeing a psychologist—it's required," and—then he suggested I might see one too. "Not mine," he declared, "but someone."

"Who?" I asked.

"I know of three psychologists in the Bay Area that work with transsexuals." Jack answered. "Check the internet."

I had already discovered there were no books on the subject at the San Francisco Public Library, and a trip to UCSF's medical library only provided information in medical terms as 'gender dysphoria' or, DSM-5. Borders, Union Square, the most complete bookstore in San Francisco, had also yielded nothing. *What do you do when you love someone and he tells you this? Where do you go for answers? Friends? My friends will not understand this.* No one I knew had experienced anything like this. *Transsexual*—Not even the dictionary defined it!

What does it all mean? Jack keeps saying he doesn't want me to leave. *I love him, but how do we work through this? Can we work through this? Do I leave? Do I stay? If I stay, how do I support him? If I stay, what does it mean to me?* Clearly, I had no direction. So, I took Jack's suggestion, went on the internet, and found a psychologist I hoped might be able to help me understand.

* * *

I pressed the small black button on the dull brass doorplate and heard a small bell ring somewhere in the

130

distant interior. Soon a buzz accompanied a click and I turned the doorknob and pushed the door. Her instructions had been clear. "Just step inside and take a seat. I will be expecting you."

It was a simple room designed in a style of yesteryear. I sat in a small wicker chair pillowed in a dark brown fabric. I noted a burgundy chaise lounge stretched along the far wall, *a psychiatrist's couch*, I thought. I pondered how many souls had lain upon it and poured out their own life stories to a listening ear.

The room was quiet except for the sound of a ticking wall clock, which made me more aware of my own frayed nerves. I consoled myself knowing that our conversation would be confidential.

I glanced about the room, looking for a sign of reassurance that this woman might understand my predicament. Magazines lay on the table. The issues of *People, Sunset, and Sports Illustrated* were new, but did not provide the consolation I needed.

I assumed that she would understand Jack's thinking, but I also hoped that she would also be able to understand mine.

"I have had no one to talk to," I had stated over the phone. "I'm hoping you might help me understand what's happening. I have so many questions, and I need to talk about how I feel. I need help finding answers--show me which way to go." I was Alice in Wonderland, inquiring of the Cheshire Cat.

I had been making every effort to wrap my mind around the concept of Jack's decision, but without anyone with whom to discuss my concerns, I could not sort out my feelings.

"Face it, Diane, you don't want me to do this," Jack had said angrily, and in this he was right. In my perfect world, this wouldn't be my choice. He viewed my questions as a rejection of him, but in that he was wrong. I just didn't understand and I had no compass to guide me. I didn't know what to say to Jack to prove that his decision made no difference in the feelings I had for him. There was no question that I wanted him to be happy, but it raised a lot of questions as to what would become of us?

Without information, without answers, I was unable to support Jack in the way he needed, nor did I know how to navigate a way through for myself. What was clear was that, if Jack couldn't talk to me about it, I had to find help elsewhere.

I held my list of questions in a tight grip and renewed my determination not to let my emotions take over. I could not forget what I felt was important to ask, but I knew that the sense of relief at being able to talk about my situation, was already forcing my emotions to the surface. The cost of the session was $250 an hour and Jack had not offered to help pay for it, so I needed to make sure that I made every minute count.

I wasn't sure what to expect and feeling awkward about how to start, I said nothing. The middle-aged woman of medium frame, with short blonde hair that fluffed about a kind face, smiled. Our polite introductions exchanged, she settled back into an over-stuffed armchair and looked at me expectantly as I sat on the edge of the small sofa.

"Where should I start?" I asked. The clock had started to tick. I nervously began to unfold the sheet of paper, which held my list of questions.

She must have sensed my reluctance to expose my fears, and so she broke the ice herself.

"When you called for the appointment you said that your significant other had revealed his secret desire to become a woman. You were hoping I could answer some questions for you?" Her non-judgmental tone set me at ease. "You can ask whatever you wish, and I will do my best to answer. I can tell you up front that not much is known about the phenomena. While I've several transgender clients, it's rare that a significant other comes in. How long have you known?"

"The truth? Only a few weeks," I replied. Then I poured out my story. First, Jack at the top of the stairs dressed as a Diva. Then, the shock of his confession and his anger at my reaction. I spoke of my initial fears and his recent strange behavior as well as my longing to understand, and my desire to prove to Jack that even in my confusion, my feelings for him had not changed. She sat quietly and listened. Her eyes revealed her compassion for me and understanding for Jack.

"I hardly know what to say," she admitted finally. "I have to give you credit because you are very unusual. It hasn't been my experience that a significant other is willing to stay. Usually, there is no desire to understand the phenomena, or to show empathy for it. Psychiatry terms the condition gender dysphoria, but I have personally come to the conclusion through my practice that as psychologists, we are not looking at a psychological illness but a 'mismatch' of nature. No definitive studies have been done in the U.S., but based on what *is* known, it is likely there are several hundred thousand transgendered persons in the U.S. But it may take years before anyone truly understands the transgender phenomena. Do you love Jack?"

"Yes," I answered without reservation.

"You love him for the person he is—the person you know?" she asked.

I nodded.

"You said that Jack wants to go forward—sex reassignment surgery eventually?"

"He has talked about it, yes . . . ." I stammered, finding it difficult to acknowledge it as fact.

"Keep in mind that as Jack changes and his new persona emerges, the Jack you know, may die. I was prepared to help you deal with the process of grief over the loss of Jack."

"What do you mean?" I asked.

"As I said, not a lot is known. You said Jack is taking hormones?"

"Yes, on and off for the past couple of years," I answered.

"It's not uncommon for transsexuals to begin hormone therapy before coming out to friends and loved ones. Some begin them in secret to see what changes take place, to help them decide if it's really what they want. Then, they might stop out of fear that someone will discover their secret before they, themselves, are willing to share their secret with the world. Hormones, in this case estrogen, will have a powerful effect not only on him physically, but also emotionally and psychologically. Hormone therapy for the transgender is a new science; we don't have all of the answers yet. No doubt you know how hormones can affect you at 'that time of month?' It's likely that for Jack, it may be even more intense."

"Emotional outbursts?" I remembered Jack's crazy behavior.

"Yes, changes in mood and in temperament," she answered.

"Anger?"

"You've experienced it?" She looked concerned.

"Yes, it was frightening. I wondered if he had gone mad."

"His moods may become unpredictable. With hormone therapy in its experimental phase, finding the correct balance can be difficult. What is known, is that with adjustments things will level out over time."

It *was* the hormones! I felt reassured.

134

"His sexual feelings, his desire or responsiveness, may also fluctuate. You might notice that Jack seems depressed, more tired and irritable than usual."

"He's very much into himself. I don't know where I stand with him. He says he doesn't want me to leave him, but . . ." I thought about his menacing behavior that night at Green Apple Books and how scared I was, and shook my head, acknowledging she had hit the nail on the head.

"Keep in mind," she began, "that as Jack's persona changes, and he identifies with being female, the Jack you have known, may not be the person *she* becomes. Identity is at the core. At this point, we cannot know who Jack will be on the other side of this transformation. Often, once a person begins their transformation, they most likely will focus solely on self. As their self-integration hones their new persona, their interests can shift it to new passions, or new people. Life experiences they could only dream about prior to their transformation become possible."

"What you are suggesting is that after seven years with this man, I never even knew him!" I stated this bluntly, recognizing a reality I knew I needed to consider.

"It's a possibility," she answered. "You will have to wait and see. Do you have children?"

"We don't, but I do." I said.

"Have you spoken to them yet?" she asked. "Do they know?"

"No," I stated. "I didn't think it was a good idea, until I knew more. How could I explain something to them I didn't understand myself?"

"That's understandable," she nodded in agreement.

In the distance, a doorbell rang, interrupting the session. I panicked as I realized that this expensive hour was drawing to a close. She glanced at her watch.

"I'd like to share a final thought with you. As you embark on this journey with Jack, keep what I am about to say in mind and perhaps it will help your perspective. View it not as stages of grief, but stages of change. Some of these you have already experienced: denial, anger, bargaining, depression, and eventually comes acceptance. Be prepared for Jack to experience his own fluctuations from exuberance to grief. What all of this will mean to your relationship is impossible to predict. You have no reservation, and you are willing to work at maintaining your relationship, but much of whether this will work for the two of you will depend on Jack."

I thanked her and handed her a check before she led me from her office to the door that would lead me out to the hustle and bustle of California Street.

"Diane, I hope I've been able to give you a bit of guidance that will help you sort out some of your feelings. I wish you well. Let me know if I can be of help to you in the future." She took my hand in hers and gave it a warm squeeze.

"One more thing," she said. "Have you heard of James Morris —now, Jan Morris?"

"No, I haven't," I said.

"A pioneer in transsexualism, with wife Elizabeth they stayed together and made their relationship work. So, it *is* possible."

"Thank you," I said again, as I descended the worn steps of the Victorian. I raised my hand in a final wave goodbye and realized I still held tight in my hand the list of questions, crumpled, damp, and unanswered.

Chapter 24

Coming Out

While the visit to the psychologist had provided insight to some of my questions, and supported the idea that anything was possible, there still loomed the Big Question: *Should I stay, or should I go?* My cell phone rang, transporting me from past memories into the present.

"Hello?"

"Diane?" It was Tara. "Len needs me to stay and help with the meeting. I don't know if I will make it back," she said, her annoyance evident. "I want to hear what happened, can we catch up later?"

"Of course," I said. As the call ended, I knew I had left her with a cliffhanger and I was left riding the memory loop.

I would explain to Tara that I stayed because I knew for what my heart hoped and I was determined to be supportive of Jack. I wanted to see where the journey took us. We agreed we didn't want to lose each other. Knowing it had worked for others, I held tight to the idea that love conquers all.

I looked around at the nearly empty North Beach restaurant, and decided to finish off my Coca-Cola before beginning the eight-block walk to BART for the long ride home. I took out a pen and flipped through the pages of the manuscript I had shared with Tara, making a note to myself where I had left off. *We haven't even gotten to the good stuff,* I thought, as I began to read through what I had written.

As I glanced through the manuscript, my eye caught Jack's explanation of the transition process from male to female. He had explained not only what he wanted to do, but what was actually required before someone could have sex reassignment surgery.

"Age isn't a factor at fifty-two," Jack had explained. "There are medical risks like any surgical procedure. The procedures: electrolysis for facial hair removal, breast augmentation, hormones, and the genital reconstructive surgery—each have their costs and will be expensive. Insurance won't cover, so it's going to all be out-of-pocket.   There are health risks, but it's doable.   A year of psychotherapy with a licensed practitioner is required.   I am doing that now. Eventually, a psychologist's letter of recommendation to have sex reassignment surgery in the form of a written comprehensive evaluation is needed, as well as a second expert opinion from a medical physician. All in due time, but for now, first things first."

Jack was seeing a psychotherapist, had begun electrolysis, and was taking hormones. It had been a trial run before, but now it was serious. His next step, was to go public.

"For at least a year prior to surgery, I need to interact as a female in real life situations, to learn what living life as a woman will be like," he said.

He meant to dress as a female—not in a private club, or under cover of darkness, but in the light of day. *The world can be unforgiving*, I thought, and I wondered *what his patients, friends, and family that knew him, knew us, would think.* I had asked Jack about his vision of himself as female, but he had never answered. Did he really know what he was facing?

"I'll start dressing on weekends first," Jack said. "It will be fun—we can go out shopping! Dinner and plays, too. I've been wanting to see *Miss Saigon*. Eventually, I'll need to dress as a female continuously, even at work." Turning suddenly solemn, he nervously cleared his throat. This was my clue that he was still anxious and uncertain.

Jack had gone out to parties dressed in drag, it had been make-believe, not real life. He enjoyed dressing up and the attention it got him when he did. The S&M community had also given him the opportunity to experience the exchange of power between men and women through role-play. But it wasn't real life. Jack was used to the prestige of his profession, a six-figure income, and the power he had as a male in society. *What happened if all of that disappeared?* I wondered what his reality would become once he underwent the changes he was considering. I wanted Jack to be happy, but was this really the answer?

And what about me? Was I ready for this? I had never been focused on prestige, money, or power. Could we have a normal life?

* * *

"Next weekend I'll 'dress' and we can drive to Santa Cruz. We can go shopping and maybe take a walk on the beach!" Jack suggested.

I'm not ready, my inner voice said.

My mind of reason countered, y*ou have to start some time. Try for Jack's sake.*

I took a deep breath and reassured myself. *It'll be safe enough. Santa Cruz is far away from San Francisco and we won't run into anyone we know.*

Jack met me half-dressed at the door and announced he had changed his mind about Santa Cruz. "It's a woman's prerogative, you know!" Instead, he insisted we go to the Contemporary Women's Art Fair at Fort Mason.

Having anticipated a walk on the beach and a stroll through shops on the Santa Cruz pier, my flip-flops, cut-off blue jeans and Sausalito Art Fair T-shirt were no match for Jack. Dressed in a stylish white blouse wrapped tightly around a budding figure rounded out by hormones and given the added fullness of a Victoria's Secret fully-padded bra, he had disguised his maleness with well-wrapped surgical tape before wiggling into a pair of tight-fitting, size 28, Guess blue jeans. I watched and waited as he applied final touches to his already perfectly applied makeup, and pulled a platinum blonde wig over his tight-fitting skullcap. He preened, shook his head, flounced and fluffed boldly and then practiced the smile he referred to as a naughty look as he coyly admired his womanly reflection in the bathroom mirror. Finally, he slipped into a pair of bright pink Converse tennis shoes and announced, "I'm ready. Let's go!"

I suddenly found myself hesitating, dumbstruck. I was not ready for this.

"Are you sure you don't want to go to Santa Cruz?" I pleaded, hoping to persuade him to take Door Number One. "It's a perfect day for the beach."

"Don't you think I'll pass?" Jack asked, looking for reassurance, while ignoring my suggestion and my discomfort.

In previous conversations, I had spoken with Jack about what the average woman wears in any given situation. How she would consider the weather, the function, and the company she would keep before choosing an outfit. Social conditioning and the nuances women learned while growing up were lost on someone who had lived for fifty-plus years as a man.

"You might consider changing your wig—maybe a different color?" I suggested, knowing that he had several others.

Jack received my suggestion with a pout, grabbed his purse off of a table, and headed for the door. "Today I'm Jocelyn, but you can call me Joss," he announced.

"Jocelyn?" I asked, taken back by surprise, but knowing Jack had been struggling with this decision. "You've decided on a name?"

"For today, I will try it out. I am still considering," Jocelyn, flashes her I-have-the-right-to-change-my-mind smile. "And check your pronouns," she reminded me. "It's she or her, not he or him," she added, her eyes giving me a or-I'll-drop-you-in-your-tracks stare.

I was having difficulty with the duplicity of Jocelyn.

Driving through the city with the top down on the small red convertible, I realized Jocelyn, the sexy driver, had no lack of interest from male motorists she passed.

At the art fair, I noticed a few men and women looked at 'her' with curiosity, but most did not pay attention enough to notice. This reassured me, because if anyone questioned us, I did not know how I would handle it. I continued to worry about running into someone we knew. I was not up for questions or a confrontation.

After an hour of perusing the artists' stalls, Jocelyn pulled me aside. "I'm hungry," she whispered, "Would you go get me something to eat?"

Her request, along with the frightened look on her face, made me pause.

"What's wrong?" I asked.

141

"My voice, the food vendor will know I'm a man when I try to speak." Her expression changed from fear, to anger. "I don't sound like a female, Diane!" Upon the whine of Jocelyn's male voice, some people nearby looked at us curiously. Jack had practiced controlling his voice by speaking in a higher pitch, but in this stressful situation, it was clear he had not mastered the technique. He grew pale and began to tremble.

"It's okay, I'll get us something to eat. Wait here," I assured her.

As I left to purchase a muffin and a Diet Coke, Jocelyn seemed to shrink back into the wall. But when I returned, she was nowhere to be found. I panicked, scrutinizing the crowd for the platinum blonde. *Where is he! What happened to her?*

Moments later, with my own anxiety at its peak, I heard a calm voice in perfect feminine pitch, say "Thank you for the Diet Coke."

"Where were you, Jack?" My voice reflected irritation and my own fright. I had voiced the unforgiveable, and called Jocelyn, Jack.

"I was in the ladies' room, Diane," Jocelyn answered, batting her eyes and smiling with the 'cat that swallowed the canary' look which had become increasingly familiar.

"The ladies' room?" I choked back my surprise. *What if he'd been discovered in the women's public restroom? No one would understand, and the action would be considered sexual perversion. Jack would be arrested and charged with public indecency!*

Jack nodded. "It's hard to pee sitting down, but I did it!"

While my own fear ran rampant making my heart race, and I tried to grapple with the potential implications of 'what if,' Jocelyn had turned her fear into a personal victory.

Chapter 25

Exotic Erotic Ball

"I'm freezing," I said, shivering from the cold. The air hung heavy with a promise of rain. As we inched along in the line that snaked around the Concourse Center at 7th and Brannon, I wondered if we would make it inside before the rain came.

Changing my position in an effort to shield myself from the cold, I huddled close to Jack, hoping he would open his jacket to shield me, and pull me in close to share the warmth of his body.

"Aren't you cold?" I asked, dropping a hint, and unable to imagine that he wasn't.

"It shouldn't be long now," Jack said ignoring me, and wrapping himself tighter into his jacket. He stepped to the side, teetering on black patent heels, and surveyed the line in both directions. There were several hundred party-goers costumed and masked in every type of get-up imaginable, from homemade to Halloween Store. "The line is starting to move," he said.

* * *

Jack's most recent surprise had been sprung a couple of weeks before as we had hamburgers at Mel's on Geary Street.

"Guess what we are doing on your birthday!" he quizzed, as he flourished two tickets towards me over a basket of fries.

"The Exotic Erotic Ball? Halloween Night?" I exclaimed.

Jack beamed, "Aren't you excited? We can get dressed up and par-taaay," he laughed.

The fact was, I wasn't sure *how* to feel. Since Jack's coming out, and his seemingly successful excursion to the Women's Art and Craft Fair in August, without any explanation he had begun to dress as a woman less and less, and in public not at all. He seemed to have settled back into being the same-ole Jack—blue jeans and sweatshirts. Jocelyn had disappeared to parts unknown. I wondered, but dared not ask, if Jack was having second thoughts? Reminding myself that only time would tell, I sensed Jack had things to figure out for himself. But deep down, I hoped that Jack had changed his mind.

"I'll have to think about what to wear," I pondered, wanting him to take the lead. "Do you have any idea about what *you* will wear?" I quizzed.

Jack took less than a second to answer. "I'm going to wear the long-sleeved silk shirt, black leather pants, and high boots. I'll go as a pirate and wear a patch over my eye," he winked. "I noticed a great pirate hat the other day in a store on Haight. I'll have to see if it's still there. You?"

"My stiletto boots, fishnets, black leather skirt," I said, realizing my scene costume was the only thing I had in my closet of make-believe. With Christmas not far off, I was financially stretched with gifts yet to be purchased for the kids. I couldn't afford to buy anything new, but I hadn't forgotten our spontaneous trip to Stormy Leather a few weeks earlier when Jack encouraged me to try on a couple of leather corsets. He knew how much I coveted one.

"I can't afford these!" I had laughed. To appease Jack, had tried them on anyway and found one in particular that we both agreed looked good on me. Begrudgingly, I put it back on the rack before we left, but I saw Jack sneak another look and examine the price tag. I sensed he was contemplating the corset as a surprise birthday gift. Now, I made a mental note to self: *I'll wear the black leather corset you are planning to surprise me with!*

* * *

The steady nudge of the crowd continued to move us forward. The crowd became more animated as the music inside reached out to us on the street. A woman on stilts, dressed in a fairy costume of garish pink and green and covered in sparkles, slowly moved along the line tossing glitter from a small bag attached at her waist, while onlookers cajoled and gawked up her skirt.

Standing amidst the many other outlandish costumes, my own was very plain. In a last-minute decision, I had decided to forego the leather skirted dominatrix look and leave the floggers at home. Instead, I wore large hoop earrings, jangly coin jewelry, fishnet stockings, and thigh-high boots. Over it all, I had pulled on a mini-skirted velveteen tunic top I had found at the Renaissance Faire a couple of years before. An item I had forgotten, then found, and stuffed to the back of my closet. It was my version of a sexy pirate girl outfit. *I'll match Jack!* I thought, wanting to look like a couple, and still holding out hope my "birthday corset" would add extra 'varoom.'

I had been disappointed when Jack hadn't come to the door when he came to pick me up. Instead, he called and asked that I meet him at the curb. As I opened the car door, I was struck by the scent of perfume. As I saw the shoulder-length red-hair, a feeling of discomfort suddenly flooded over me.

"You didn't tell me you had changed your mind about your costume," I said, getting into the car. A familiar sense of shock experienced around the party months before resurfaced and confusion began to spin as I recognized Jocelyn had reappeared.

"I thought this would be fun, Diane! It's Halloween after all, and we haven't been to the Exotic Erotic Ball before. Besides," she said with a giggle and a smile accentuated by passionate pink lipstick. "Doesn't a girl have the right to change her mind?"

I didn't know what to say. I was walking the plank.

I continued to hold my tongue as Jocelyn squirmed and shifted in her seat as she drove. Reaching inside of her jacket she fidgeted, seeming to make adjustments. I could not help but notice her discomfort, and cattily thought, *if you don't get the right fit, a bra can bind.*

* * *

"Two," Jocelyn said, as she passed the tickets to the man at the door. She pulled on my hand and we passed through the turnstile and meshed into the throng of people already inside.

"Where are we going?" I shouted over the crowd towards Jocelyn as she muscled her way towards the up escalator through sweaty leather-clad, bare-butt boys and bare-chested women that milled about.

"This way!" Jocelyn shouted back, as we passed the stage with its strobe lights, color, and blaring guitars.

I felt a man's hand slip under my skirt.

"Some guy just tried to grope me!" I shouted out in disgust, wishing for a swashbuckling pirate who would defend my honor.

146

"Just follow me!" shouted the unconcerned passionate pink lips. She grabbed onto my arm to help her keep her balance on the first of the moving steps of the up escalator, while I struggled on my own to stave off the actions of the creepy guy.

The beat of the music resounded from the first-floor stage, making conversation impossible. Jostled to and fro by the push of the crowd, we reached the upper level where Jocelyn's hand slipped from mine. Momentarily, I stopped to look over a railing and examine the crowd on the floor below. Leather-jacketed men wearing devil masks and scantily-clad women dressed in next-to-nothing, many masked in face paint, danced to the music of the zombie band near the first-floor stage.

"It looks like Mardi Gras!" I shouted to Jack, thinking he was next to me. But, Jocelyn had moved towards a side room and was making her way in.

What the heck, I thought. *Wait for me!*

As I moved towards the room, I recognized a couple I had seen at The Castle events. Another man said, "Hi, Diane!" as I approached, and another dutifully stepped aside. I recognized it then—*this is a bondage demonstration room!* I worked my way through the crowd of curious ticket-paying onlookers and seasoned voyeurs who were watching a spanking demonstration, curious as to why Jack found it necessary to make this our first stop.

Seeing her just ahead in the crowd, I heard Jack's voice call out to a short, heavy-set female dressed in a long black flowing gown standing in the middle of the room. She turned, smiled, and reached out to him, pulling Jocelyn in close.

It was Marta, the dominant that gave the bondage class I attended! I recalled, thinking she was obnoxious, and without refinement.

"You made it," she beamed.

She was expecting him—expecting Jocelyn?

No longer seeming to be aware of my presence, Jocelyn stood before Marta, with head bowed.

What the hell! I thought, as I began to flame with irritation.

Grasping both of Jocelyn's hands in hers, I watched her lips softly speak.

"Do you have it on?" she asked.

The head of auburn hair nodded.

"Show me," she commanded.

Before my startled eyes, Jocelyn slowly removed her leather jacket, and let it drop to the floor. Reaching up the back of the dress, she slowly unzipped the black spandex gown, and allowed its top to slip down to her waist. The black leather corset I had tried on at Stormy Leather fit snugly on Jocelyn's wiry frame and pinched in her already small waistline.

I gasped and felt another flush of heat as tears of disbelief and disappointment burned and threatened to spill from my eyes.

Marta saw me watching from the edge of the crowd. She smiled, and then shouted, "I have always said I wanted to see 'her' in a leather corset and wearing four-inch high heels! Thank you for helping get her here." Victory was hers.

My help? I stood speechless, my anger growing, as I felt my trust once again betrayed. I watched as Jack's alter ego re-zipped the dress.

"Jack!" I shouted, as I moved forward, shoving against the crowd. I approached the two, glared at Marta, and grabbed for his arm.

Without a word, Jocelyn turned, pushed past me, and began to work her way out of the crowded room towards the corridor. Her path blocked, I caught up to her, reached down, and grasped her buttock through

148

the black spandex of her dress. With my recently manicured, very sharp dark red nails, I pinched as hard as I could and I didn't let go.

"Keep walking, Jocelyn!" I shouted in her ear, as I transferred my frustration and my heart's pain to her derrière. Escaping the room, I sensed my overwhelming rage and released my grip. Jocelyn whined and winced in pain at the final forceful pinching squeeze, as she turned and stood with her back against a concrete wall.

"How could you?" I screamed, in words that were swallowed by the deafening crowd. "This was supposed to be *my* Birthday Night!"

Chapter 26

The Other Woman

As I stormed from the Concourse Pavilion heading for the car, Jack assured me it was nothing.

"She's a friend!" he had shouted from behind.

"She's no friend, Jack! Believe me," I growled back.

Could Marta have known back then that I was Jack's girlfriend? The thought made my stomach turn.

The first time I had seen Marta was at a breast bondage class I had attended while I was still trying to discover everything I could about S&M. A well-known dominatrix, Marta had given a demonstration with the help of her submissive partner, an unkempt man in his mid-thirties, who had tightly crisscrossed and bound Marta's large breasts, which displayed multiple tattoos and nipple piercings, with colorful yarn tied in intricate knots. It had looked painful, but Marta, dressed in a black net skirt and military combat boots, seemed undaunted.

I had dropped in and arrived late. The demonstration was over, and the attendees were milling about. I was standing at a table with leaflets and flyers about upcoming classes, when I overheard Marta mention someone named Jack.

"Jack, the next time I see you, I want you wearing *only* four-inch heels and a black leather corset with your waist bound to twenty-two inches!" Her voice peeled off in raucous laughter as a male attendee snickered.

I was put off when I heard the name. Using someone's real name in public broke the Community rules of confidentiality that were put in place to help provide a safety net for those seeking to explore their sexuality. *My client* was acceptable, but *Jack* was not. As I listened to the other attendees, I learned that Marta was considered to be an edge player, someone with a reputation of not playing by the rules. And she wore her bad attitude like a badge of honor. Not a person I would be able to respect. Giving her a closer look, I dismissed the idea that she would be anyone Jack would associate with. I reassured myself that Marta was not talking about *my* Jack.

Tonight, I had learned first-hand that Marta had no boundaries. Marta *had* been talking about my Jack. But had she known about Jocelyn then, nearly a year ago, even before *I* knew about Jocelyn? What did Jack see in Marta? I couldn't understand how he could be attracted to her. I wasn't jealous—I was confused.

Containing my anger, as I felt it turning to rage, I stopped in the middle of the parking lot, and turned to confront Jack.

"This 'friendship'—how did you meet?"

"She's in the hotline group," he stuttered.

I swallowed hard, realizing he had known her for a while. "Since before you began taking S&M classes?"

"Yes, she's also aware of my desire to transition and she has been very helpful. Tonight was just a game, Diane."

*She **does** know about Jocelyn! And, **before** I knew!* The realization only increased my anger.

"Helpful? And what do you mean by a game, Jack? You said you had no further interest in S&M." I felt as if I had been their pawn.

"I don't, not really," Jack replied matter-of-factly. "I simply fulfilled a friend's request."

"You've never mentioned this Marta before," I said, still groping for answers.

"I felt there was no need."

"No need?" I asked. "I would have thought you would have let me in on your plan, rather than put me in an uncomfortable situation. And *tonight*, of all nights!" I countered angrily. "And the corset, the trip to Stormy Leather, all a ruse so that you could buy a corset for yourself to prove something to *her*?"

"I didn't know how to pick a corset, Diane."

"That's not the point! You used me, Jack!" I said, finding it unthinkable that he could be so clueless.

"All along, I thought you were thinking of getting me the corset for my birthday!" I was barely able to hold back my tears. "You weren't thinking of me at all. What a fool I have been, nothing but a fool," I said, as the dam broke.

"No, Diane, no!" Jack said, taking me in his arms. "I'm sorry, I'm a selfish ass. You have every right to be upset with me, or, even hate me. But, it meant nothing. It really didn't. I was trying to prove something to *myself*. I took a dare. I'm sorry." Jack's contrite look told me he did not know how to atone for his sin. He handed me a tissue.

"Selfish! You're right!" I said, taking the tissue and pushing him away. "What were you trying to prove? Are you her submissive, Jack? What—she snaps her fingers and you do whatever she asks you to do?"

My mind reeled as I thought to myself, *To Marta, Jack's only a power trip, but I'm trying to have a life with him.*

153

"No, Diane! It's not that way! I can explain. It's not what you're thinking."

"What am I thinking, Jack? I'll tell you! I'm thinking that I need to leave you. Walk away right now!" I said, reaching for the car door that I found still locked. "I love you, but all of this is becoming too much. I want to support you, but . . ."

"But I haven't been honest," Jack said.

"Exactly, Jack," I said, surprised he'd admit it. "You haven't been honest from the beginning. From the time I met you, you've lied to me. And each time, I've forgiven your deception. That's where I've been a fool, Jack, believing in you enough to forgive you."

"I'm truly sorry. Please, give me another chance to prove to you that it meant nothing," Jack pleaded, unlocking the car door. "I'll do whatever you say."

"Take me home," I said, as he swung the passenger door open.

Jack tossed Jocelyn's auburn wig, skullcap and four-inch heels behind the seat before scooting into the car and turning the key in the ignition. I continued. "You need to figure out what you want. If you want to continue to have a relationship with me, start by being honest. Stop keeping things from me, Jack. You want to transition—to life as a woman? Then, do it. I don't know from one day to the next whether you will be Jack or Jocelyn. This is making me crazy. And, another thing, Jack, I don't want you to see Marta again."

I fell silent for the remainder of the drive, but I knew that even with everything that had happened, my heart had still not let Jack go.

"Can I come in, Diane," Jack asked, as we pulled up in front of my house.

"No, it's late and I am tired." I was telling a half-truth. The fact was, I worried that one of the kids might still be up.

It had been almost a year since any of my children had spent time around Jack. When Jack and I saw each other, we usually met at his flat. Each of the kids was busy with school and activities of their own. They were teens and young adults by now, and old enough to understand, but I had concluded that until Jack stopped waffling about his gender identity and had made a final decision, either for him or for her, that I would not encourage Jack/Jocelyn to be a part of their lives. Their lives had been hard enough. I could not predict how my children would react to the idea of Jack's changes, or how I would explain to them my own feelings when I was still dealing with Jack's/Jocelyn's duplicity and my own effort to determine if I should stay or I should go. I would let time march on.

Chapter 27

Out of the Mouths of Babes

During the weeks following the Exotic Erotic Ball, Jack committed to the transition of becoming female. He decided to dress the part on weekends to bolster his confidence. Finally, he decided to begin dressing as a woman full-time. With that proclamation, I knew the time had come for me to talk my kids before they, too, had an at-the-top-of-the-stairs moment. *But what would I say? What was the best way to explain the what and why of Jack's decision?*

I had gone home early because work was slow. I let the kids know I was going to make something special for dinner as a way to encourage them all to be present. The announcement would come after dinner. Once the salad and plates of spaghetti were devoured, seconds of iced tea had been poured, and cookies were on the table, I broached the subject. I might as well have been giving them their first lesson in 'where babies come from.'

"That explains a lot," my eldest son, David now twenty-two, said matter-of-factly. Getting up from the table on the pretext of helping to clear the plates away, he discretely excused himself, saying, "I hope everything works out, Mom. By the way, I have plans to go out with the guys, I'll be back later," he said, heading toward the door. Avoidance—*David must feel very uncomfortable,* I thought.

"A girl. He wants to be a girl?" Alex asked, his voice tinged with disgust. The sixteen-year-old grabbed a cookie and jumped up to follow after his older brother. "I'm going too; wait for me." I saw him shake his head and heard him snicker and comment to David as they went out the back door, "At least he's not *our* dad."

Twenty-year old Brian continued to pick and stare at his half-eaten food and look distressed.

"Can I answer any questions for any of you?" I asked the remaining three, witnessing their looks of confusion and disbelief. So far, their reactions were somewhat what I expected. Although San Francisco is known for its diversity of people and ideas, my children had lived 'vanilla' lives.

Give them time, I thought, trusting that ultimately, they might accept Jocelyn.

"Why would Jack do something like that?" Brian asked.

"It's who he feels he is," I said.

"I don't get it," Brian said. "I know it happens . . . but why him?"

"I know it's hard to understand, Brian. I had questions, too."

"He's gay then?" Brian asked.

"No, Brian, he says he's not."

"Then exactly what is he?" asked Brian.

"A guy, but not a guy," interjected eighteen-year-old Daniel, the middle child.

"That's why he didn't mind if I painted his nails pink when I was playing with my Barbie," stated Kristie, now fourteen. "I thought he was just being nice."

"He wants to answer any questions you might have," I reassured them.

"So . . . what do we call him? Or—*her*," Daniel asked. "Jackie?"

"Jocelyn," I said.

"Jocelyn—right, Okay, Jocelyn it is!" Daniel said, trying to assure me he was onboard.

"I still don't get it," Brian said as he got up from the table. He went to his room and slammed the door.

"Brian's upset," I said to the remaining two. Brian had always looked up to Jack, jokingly referring to Jack as mini-Einstein. Jack had been his go-to person for science or math questions.

"He'll be okay, Mom," Kristie assured me. "But how are you?"

Such a mature young woman for her age, I thought proudly.

"This was a shock," she said, not waiting for my reply. "None of us would ever have suspected."

"It was a surprise to me, too," I said.

"What are you going to do?" she asked.

"I don't know yet," I answered.

"He is like a dad to us, you know."

That was when I saw tears in her eyes.

"I thought he might walk me down the aisle someday," she said.

"Come here," I said, pulling her towards me and hugging her close. "It's what he feels he needs to do." *What more could I say?*

"Everybody needs to be who they are," Daniel added, showing compassion. "He'll still be the same person on the inside . . . won't he?"

"I hope so . . . we'll have to wait and see," I answered, knowing there were no guarantees.

"You taught us to have an open mind, Mom, so I'm not going to judge him." said Daniel. "But you know others will."

"Thank you, for that, Daniel," I said, acknowledging he was right, while wishing he was wrong.

Over time, each of the kids took Jack's transition to his new life in his or her own way. They were always being courteous and polite, but often not in attendance if there was pre-warning that Jocelyn might stop by.

Jack's transition was most difficult for Brian. It would be years before Brian confided in me how difficult it was for him to wrap his mind around why the 'smart science guy' who he respected and looked up to as a mentor, would choose such a difficult path in life. To Brian it wasn't about betrayal, he felt it defied all logic. After all, wasn't the sky blue and the grass green?

Chapter 28

What Women Do

As we waited for Giorgio to finish with his previous client, I picked up a hairstyle magazine and flipped through its pages.

"There, Joss!" I said, pointing to the photo of a sleek shoulder-length 'do' with flipped up ends. "That's what I mean!"

Jocelyn stared straight ahead, without giving the photo a second glance. I could tell she was apprehensive, but I had run out of ways to reassure her.

For the past six months, Jack had committed to living life as Jocelyn, and to her new role with gusto. She searched for ways to complete her vision of herself. Wearing store-bought wigs, inexpensive and made of artificial fiber, the wig color and style changed weekly and sometimes, daily. It had become evident that the store-bought wigs were unacceptable for long-term use. They were hard to manage and did not look natural. Becoming Jocelyn with a full head of hair, when Jack was a fine-haired, balding male, had presented its own puzzling dilemma. Her decision to invest in a hairpiece made of actual human hair was a milestone commitment in her transition. After a great deal of investigation into what might work best, a choice was made. Dark-haired Jack would become strawberry-blond, shoulder-length haired Joss.

"It's expensive," she said, "but its real hair! Feel how fine the texture is?"

"A girl has to do what a girl has to do," I agreed, as I examined the texture of what was purported to be fine Caucasian hair. "If it holds up as promised, the investment will have been well worth it."

After a $1,800 credit card swipe and four hours on a Saturday morning to glue and weave the hairpiece by an 'invisible blend' method, it was put in place. Jocelyn's decision had resulted in a full head of luxurious hair. Assured that the new hair would last up to three years before needing replacement, and six-to-eight weeks before needing to be reapplied, Joss had gone in feeling confident about her choice and hopeful for a beautiful result.

Waiting as the feminine tresses were attached, I too had great expectations. However, on first view, it was evident that some styling tips and some taming of the flyaway mane that had the appearance of newly-mown hay, was badly needed. Viewing the technician's own hairstyle, I felt she was not the person to consult.

Once in Jocelyn's tiny red car for the drive back to the city from San Mateo, I watched as she re-combed, tweaked, fluffed, and flounced using her rearview mirror.

"Do you like it?" I finally dared to ask.

"I like the color," she said, as she preened. "Maybe I should have gotten a shorter cut—more like yours," she said, before falling silent.

Clearly, Jocelyn was not happy.

"I have an idea," I said, as I thought of my own stylist. "Why don't I give Giorgio a call? My treat, in honor of your new hair," I offered. "Besides being a

162

wonderful stylist, he's such a great person, he will be supportive. I know he could suggest products to tame it down. He can even up any straggly ends and, if you decide, maybe do a trim. At the least, he can give you styling tips for everyday living."

Joss' first real salon experience, I thought, happy I had suggested it. Since she had gone forward with the transition, I found myself enjoying what I could share with Joss, and felt I found a niche particularly when it was something women do with dress, hair, and make-up. It was especially fun if I could contribute with something she had never tried.

"I think you would love what Giorgio could do with your hair," I tried to reassure her. A trip to Berkeley was planned.

* * *

"Hi! You two! It's sooo nice to see you both!" Giorgio said, as he strutted lightly around the room. Walking directly to Jocelyn, he motioned for her to stand, took her by the hand and twirled her about, scrutinizing her hair.

"Hmmmm . . . I see Diane finally managed to convince you to come see me! Good! Let's see what we can do." Giorgio's green eyes flashed his approval as he winked at me.

"It's sooo important for you to have a natural look at this stage of your transition!" He said, as he led Joss to his stylist's chair, and tossed a protective garment around her. "Big hair! That's a mistake that way too many people make!"

"So . . . what would you like me to do?" Giorgio asked. "It appears you need a trim, and Diane mentioned you might like it styled? I can easily take care of the dry appearance."

Jocelyn sat looking frightened. *She's overwhelmed*, I thought, and I quickly took the initiative to give Giorgio a response.

"Giorgio, perhaps you could start by trimming the straggly ends, and evening up the bangs. Then Joss can decide if she wants to have you shorten it," I asserted. "We are open to suggestions."

Giorgio circled the chair, scrutinizing and feeling strands of Joss' hair.

"Your hair has an artificial look and feel, but you said it was human hair?" Giorgio asked, appearing dubious. "There is a quick test for that," he said. Without waiting for an answer, he plucked a hair from its base, and lit a match to it.

"Hmmm, well that tells me what to do next," he said, and without further explanation the "Master" began to snip and shape.

"There! Now the hair will hold its style!" He moved back, reaching for a flat iron and a spray bottle that sat on a nearby counter, and asked, "What do you think?"

Jocelyn sat without answering, or moving, her eyes closed shut.

Without further ado, Giorgio grasped the shoulder length strands of hair, sprayed each section before placing it between the blades of the hot iron. A slight sizzle and steam rose at each stroke, and with each motion the out-of-control took shape as each tress took on a smoothness and a glow of color and light, that outwardly reflected vitality and life.

"There! There you are! Your hair is finished. Now—what do you think?" asked Giorgio, obviously pleased with his effort. He stood back and admired his Edward Scissorhands 'do'.

Jocelyn opened her blue-green eyes and stared at the reflection in the mirror. A slow smile of approval crossed her face melting away the look of fear.

"I like it!" she purred, as she held the mirror in her hand and spun herself in the chair to look at her reflection from different angles.

"Joss! Your hair—it's beautiful!" I said, unable to hold back my amazement. "You look sensational!" I said with admiration, as I realized Giorgio had transformed the harsh appearance of the unruly mane into begging-to-be-touched tresses of feminine sensuality.

"You saw how I did it?" questioned Giorgio of Jocelyn, as he proceeded to take the next few minutes to give specific instructions on how to achieve the look and make sure she understood. "These are the products you will need, and here is the name of the flat iron you need to get," Giorgio explained, as he placed the items in a pink shopping bag. "Sleep on the silk pillow case—my compliments," he said, smiling as he tossed a small flat pink package into the bag. "Your hairstyle will stay in place for at least a week. You won't have to do a thing. Just run a comb through it and you'll be good to go. It will stay just like this until you wash your hair next time. If you have any issue please give me a call," he offered.

Giorgio handed Jocelyn the bag along with his card, as I passed Giorgio a check for a job well done.

We left Giorgio's studio and stepped out into the darkness of evening. Joss' hair shimmered with star-like glints from the glow of the streetlights.

"I'm speechless, Joss!" I said, as I watched her hair, stirred by the evening breeze, float lightly about, creating a halo of light and framing her face in softness. "Your hair—*you* look beautiful."

If any doubt remained that Jack could pass as a female, all doubt has been erased with this stunning magical transformation, I thought.

Acting smug, Joss seemed pleased that she had made another leap forward in her womanly transition. I smiled to myself, excited about having been able to play a part in showing her something that women do. The next morning, however, as the clock struck 6:00 a.m., Jocelyn awoke and started her day as usual. The *Cinderella* spell broke as she got up, took a shower, and washed her hair.

Chapter 29

Marcella

I always enjoyed the BART ride from Daly City to my evening class at San Francisco State's downtown location, because it gave me time to think. As the train sped towards the Embarcadero Street Station, I closed my eyes to the hum of its rails and found my mind adrift, thinking about time that seemed to have flown by.

Jack had been living as Jocelyn full-time for over a year. Sex reassignment surgery was planned for February 2000, just five months away. I no longer referred to Jack as Jack, but as Jocelyn. I had learned to wrap my mind around her changing persona. The name had stuck, and the finality of it came once the necessary legal paperwork had been accomplished. *What's in a name?* My thoughts seemed to twist and bounce: in name he was a she, but it hadn't kept me from seeing the Jack I knew in everything she did. The sense of humor and wit, interests, intelligence, and the outlook towards life had not changed. I remained hyper-aware of the need not to offend, so I found myself constantly on guard and continually checking myself. *Not him*, I thought, *her*.

Caught up in the planning of sex reassignment surgery and the physical changes that would entail, Jack seemed to have given little thought to other inevitable changes that would come as a result. First, and foremost, the transition to her was ruining his business. Jack's patients weren't as accepting of Jocelyn as Jack and I had hoped. Jocelyn was forced to close two of three offices, and, unable to keep up the mortgage on the Pacific Heights Victorian, sold it and opted to move to Sausalito. Without question, she was hurting financially and had begun considering her medical practice job options and how to reinforce her income.

Never far from my own thoughts were still questions about how the transition would ultimately affect our life as a couple, and how aspects of our sexual relationship would change. I realized it was transition without negotiation, but I also knew physical changes were permanent, and that there would be no going back. All the same, I needed to prepare for my own part of what was coming, and I knew it would be without Jack's, or rather, without Jocelyn's, help.

Society would view us differently: *Two women living together in a relationship would be considered lesbians. As a heterosexual woman, was I prepared for that label and perhaps that lifestyle?* As for sex, I rationalized that minus certain body parts and with the addition of others, *she would still be the same person on the inside*—Jack, the person I loved. But I couldn't keep from wondering that when Jack was in a female body, *would my feelings be different? What about my needs?*

Eyes closed, lost in thought, I had not noticed the tall, shorthaired woman with a boyish demeanor edge her way towards me.

"Hi sweetie!" My eyes flew open at recognition of the familiar voice, and I glanced up to see the flash of a flirtatious smile. In a red plaid shirt and denim bib overalls, she stood over me, gripping the overhead handrail for balance as she swayed with the motion of the train. Marcella called everyone sweetie.

"Hi!" I responded, taking in her radiant smile and sparkling eyes.

"You think we'll make it to class on time?" she asked, with a soft throaty laugh.

"I doubt it," I said, as I caught her eyes betray her thoughts. She gave me the once-over I had only seen in the eyes of men. Embarrassed by her scrutiny, I avoided eye contact by glancing at my watch.

"Only something short of a miracle will get us to class on time," I said.

To my relief, our conversation was cut short as we entered an underground tunnel. In the reflection of the train's window, I watched her watch me with curiosity. She possessed a unique energy I found disquieting.

When the train stopped, I rose quickly. Marcella steadied her book bag and stepped toward the door.

"Excuse us!" she shouted, "Coming through!"

Holding back a horde of exiting BART riders with her command, she opened my path of escape. "Before you!" she insisted. Shooting a grateful look in her direction, I stepped onto the platform and moved away from the crowd.

"We're late!" I exclaimed, quickening my pace toward the exit.

Marcella followed closely, walking jauntily, with a demeanor of cockiness. "I bet I get there before you do," she teased. With a half-laugh, she pushed past me on the escalator, flashed a mischievous grin and disappeared through the crowd towards the 495 Market Street Building.

I considered Marcella articulate, upbeat, and bright—the smartest in our class. She knew her business.   A dynamo of a negotiator, she knew employment law forward and backward, and could argue and win any case without missing a beat. We had several classes in common, and we had worked together on various projects. She made no secret of the fact that she worked for a woman-owned business that promoted alternative life styles. With both of us attending evening classes at SFSU, I had interacted with her enough to realize she was a warm, compassionate and caring person. I had entertained the thought of our being friends, but this likelihood seemed doubtful. We were worlds apart. The boyish style and rough exterior that added to her charm, also gave her away. She was gay.

The class dragged on. I shifted my weight on the hard, wooden chair, but I could not concentrate. My mind constantly wandered back to Jocelyn and the changes that were inevitable. *How would I handle my new role once Jocelyn's physical transition was complete?*

"We'll be taking a fifteen-minute break."   The instructor's announcement penetrated through my mind fog. As the class moved towards the door, Marcella approached.

"You okay?" Her voice reflected a look of concern.

My heart skipped a beat. *Somehow, she must know*, I thought. I sensed my own paranoia.

"I was trying to get your attention during class," she snickered. "I even threw a pencil at you when the instructor wasn't looking. You didn't even notice!"

I smiled at her attempt to humor me.

"I'm fine," I lied. "It's been a long day. I'm just tired and can't concentrate."

"I'm going with friends for coffee after class. I thought you might like to join us," she suggested.

I hesitated, surprised at the invitation. "Thanks, but I should be getting home."

"Come on! It'll be fun. I'm taking BART to my sister's in San Bruno this evening. Don't you go that way?"

She'd noticed?

"We can ride BART to Daly City together," she continued, "I promise we won't stay late."

There was the smile again—friendly, accepting, comforting—and somehow, captivating. I felt an inexplicable connection.

"Okay, why not?" I said. *Besides*, I thought, *it will give me a chance to get out with others.* Since Jack's decision had become public, I felt isolated from friends. They no longer called, or when they did, they only sought answers to their curious questions. I felt they were judging me. Why is she staying with Jack? Poor thing. Didn't she know he was gay? I'd become food for gossip.

After class ended, we walked across the street to Peet's. I searched for a table while Marcella ordered our coffee. I saw her on her cell phone.

"Enrique called. They can't make it!" She stated on her return to the table. She placed a coffee in front of me and straddled a chair, leaning her forearms over its back.

"So . . . what's your story?" She asked. "I've wanted to get to know you better, but we've never had a chance to talk." Her dark brown eyes had glints of gold and looked straight at me. We talked about class, our motivations, and our eventual goals.

"I wish you could have met my friends tonight. I think you would like them," Marcella finally said. "Mara and Enrique have been together for a long time. Leanne and Judy, you'd like them, too. We're all close, more so now that Enrique's going through his transition. We're our own support group!"

Did I hear her say transition?

She continued, not knowing she had struck a chord.

"It's complicated, but we want him to be happy," she continued.

"Transition?" I asked. *Male to female? Female to male?* I wondered.

She shifted uncomfortably in her seat, as if she had inadvertently revealed something she wasn't ready to explain.

"Yeah, she's becoming a man!" She glanced at me awkwardly as if checking my reaction. "I've always wanted to be a guy, but I've never considered doing what Enrique's doing!"

Enrique was a female, transitioning to male!

I saw a trace of sadness and confusion cross her face and, in that moment, I felt an even deeper connection.

Then, there was the smile again. Her cover-up, I understood. She reached for her book bag.

"We need to get going," she said, abruptly ending our conversation.

Walking towards BART, there was an uneasy silence. I knew I had to tell her, and I didn't want to lose the opportunity.

"Marcella," I began uneasily, gathering my courage. "I know we don't know each other very well, but we have more in common than you think."

Marcella stopped and looked at me. "I already know you aren't gay!" She laughed, but became solemn when she noticed the tears in my eyes.

"My lover is transitioning too," the words spilled out. "He wants to be a woman. I don't understand it and I don't know what to do. I'm frightened about what is going to happen to us, and what it will mean to our relationship. How can I be supportive? I'm trying, but everything is changing. He says his feelings for me won't change, but I'm not the one changing. He is and I don't know if I can handle it. I want to, but I don't know what to expect."

By the look on Marcella's face as I spilled out my story, I knew *I* had struck a chord with her. She dropped her book bag and encircled me in her arms.

"Hush!" she soothed.

"We've lost our friends and everything is changing," I said, stepping back. "People will think we're lesbians. I don't know how we'll fit in. I don't know if I can change the way I need to, and I don't have anyone to talk to about it. I'm sorry, but no one I know understands what I am experiencing. Somehow, I sense you might."

"Sweetie, I'm so sorry." She pulled me towards her again, holding me in a close protective embrace. She released me but kept hold of my hand. Marcella picked up her book bag and led me towards BART train.

"I have an idea," she said matter-of-factly, as we reached the train. "There's a party Friday night. Come with me. You'll have fun. You can relax and we can talk more. I'll introduce you to my friends. I like you and they will too. You're worried about fitting in, and how you will be viewed? I've been a part of the lesbian community for over ten years. Let me show you what life is like in *my* world. I'll tell you anything you want to know."

That was the beginning of our affair.

Chapter 30

Dinner for Two

Marcella called the next day and asked if I would meet her for dinner at The Sausage Factory, an Italian restaurant in the Castro before we attended her friend's party. That Friday night, Jocelyn had her own plans, so I did not have to explain that I was planning to meet a friend. When I arrived at the restaurant, I found Marcella waiting.

"Hi, Sweetie," she said, as she sauntered over. She took my hand and guided me through the crowded seating area to the bar in the back.

"Michael, your best bottle of Shiraz," she called out to the bartender with a wink at me, as she fished a credit card out of the back pocket of her blue jeans. She waved aside my attempt to pay in part, and placed the card on the bar, never letting go of my hand.

Grasping the bottle in her free hand, she held it high as a signal to the maître d' that we were ready. Rather than seating us in the main room, he led us along a narrow corridor bordered by high-backed booths that promised quiet and privacy.

"Thanks, Paul," she said slipping him a bill.

"You don't find too many places like this anymore," she commented, as we slid into the red leather-seated booth. "I come here for the ambiance, though the food's great, too," she said, reaching for the two short glasses and filling them to the brim with Shiraz.

"Cheers!" she said, smiling, and motioning with her glass, "to new adventures."

"To new adventures," I said, raising my glass.

"So how are you doing?" she asked, her face reflecting her concern.

"I'm fine," I answered.

"No, you're not. If you were, you wouldn't be here." She smiled a knowing smile.

She's right, I thought, *I probably wouldn't*.

"Didn't you say you had questions?" she asked, with a steady gaze.

I wanted to be upfront with Marcella, but I couldn't have felt more awkward not knowing where to start.

"You said you know I am not gay," I said, stating the obvious first. "That said, my connection to the gay community is only through friends at work and a fringe group Jack and I joined. I really know nothing about the lesbian community. One concern I have is that I won't fit in and in particular, that I won't fit into the social scene."

"Ahhh . . . and just what do you think the lesbian social scene is?" Her look said she was not only perplexed, but amused.

I hoped she was not making fun of me.

"I'm not sure," I said. "But a Castro party lifestyle comes to mind—like tonight. I've never been much of a party person. I have five kids, so I'm more of a stay-at-home-person."

Marcella gave a low whistle of surprise at the disclosure.

"Since beginning her transition, Jocelyn has talked about more involvement in the community and going out more to parties in the Castro. I think she really wants to go, but I'm not sure if that's really me."

"That's it?" Marcella asked incredulously. "That's what you worried about? Parties? I thought it would be s-e-x!"

She laughed hard when I blushed, but, sensing my discomfort, reined herself in. "Seriously, I do go out a lot—but I'm single. That's Friday and Saturday nights. During the week I'm in bed by nine. I have to remember I'm not as young as I was once and my body won't take it. I don't do drugs. Well, once I tried ecstasy with some friends. It felt good, but I knew I couldn't make it a habit. I'll drink a couple of beers," she said, as she poured us another glass of wine. "And—I prefer wine when I am talking with friends."

"I know you get the party idea from everything you see on TV, and I have to admit, San Francisco is a happening place for those in the gay community," Marcella continued. "But you and Joss are a couple. Of the couples I know, a few party, but most stay home, have movie nights with their kids, an occasional dinner out, or friends in. Mara and Enrique are stay-at-home types. If I want them to go to a party, I have to drag them there. I know there's a lot of hype about gay culture, but we're just people, Diane."

I let what Marcella had to say sink in as I swirled wine in my glass.

"What you said . . . there's more," I said, hesitating, unsure whether to share the thought. "There's Pride, with a capital 'P,' and involvement in the community and the culture. While I support the community in gay rights, non-discrimination and the freedom to marry, and participate in the annual AIDS Walk, I do it because I feel it is the right thing. It is not a cause for me. For most gays or lesbians who I know, the community is an all-consuming focus. My focus is on living life, not living a cause."

I was relieved when Marcella nodded as if she understood.

"You mentioned sex? My initial attraction to Jack wasn't about sex; it was his intelligence, and the friendship and companionship we found together. Sex wasn't the initiating factor. It's been great having a relationship with a man that wasn't focused entirely on sex. Considering what's happening now, it's totally ironic."

"You *were* attracted to Jack?" Marcella asked, once the irony of the situation had sunk in.

"Not in the way I am generally attracted to men," I said.

"And how would that be?" Marcella asked, showing she was curious.

"Hot steamy passion," I said, not looking her in the eye, then quickly returning to the subject, "so maybe you can understand that while I support someone being their authentic self, and I cannot imagine going through life pretending to be someone you're not, let's face it, I'm not lesbian, transgender, or even bisexual. I'm heterosexual, but people may assume I am a lesbian because I'm with Jocelyn."

"Is that so bad?" Marcella broke the mood with a flirtatious smile.

"I don't want to pretend to be something I'm not. In all seriousness, I want to support Jocelyn in being her authentic self, but sometimes it seems that in order to do that, I may have to give up being who *I* am."

Marcella's expression stiffened and her eyes flashed.

"First, you shouldn't care what other people think. And as far as those judging your relationship, that's between you and Jocelyn. What you do behind closed doors is your business. And as for being someone you aren't? I see a woman who loves her partner. That's who you are. That's the reality of it. That's what I see and others will see it too. And, if they don't, fuck 'em!"

As her temper cooled, her smile returned.

"I understand your concern, the situation certainly isn't what you originally signed up for, but I think you worry too much," she said, opening the menu. "Let's eat. The party starts in an hour."

With dinner and another bottle of wine, the party was forgotten and Marcella didn't seem to mind. Talking, laughing, and listening to oldies on the dial-a-tune jukebox at our table, Marcella exuded a sense of lighthearted playfulness. She even lip-synched Andy Williams crooning *Moon River*. She was a free spirit and I enjoyed being in her presence. I relaxed, exhilarated by her openness as she shared with me vignettes of her lesbian life, of women loved and lost. All too soon, Paul stopped by the table with the check and to tell us that the restaurant was about to close.

Upon leaving the restaurant, I stumbled. Marcella laughed.

"Sweetie! You're a bit tipsy," she said, taking my hand. I felt awkward, as she held tight, but no one else on Castro Street seemed to notice as we made our way onto 18th to where I had parked.

"I can't drive home now. I have to wait this out," I said. The alcohol warmed my skin as the cold night air chilled me. I shivered.

"I was thinking the same thing, Sweetie," she said, as I felt her arms go around me.

"Here, sit down!" Marcella motioned to a bench in front of Chaps, a shop that catered to the district's boy crowd. Blocking the breeze by enveloping me in her coat, she held me close. Huddled together for warmth, as I sobered up enough to drive home, we talked of silly things. We made fun of the passersby like schoolgirls and planned our next meeting.

On the drive home, I marveled at the feeling of closeness we had shared. I remembered the warmth of her breath on my cheek in the night's cold air. I tried to analyze my feelings for the free-spirited woman with whom I had discovered a heartfelt connection. Our brief association was unlike any other I'd experienced with any of my women friends—we came from such different worlds. Besides her openness and willingness to trust and provide friendship, I sensed an attraction—not sexual, but sensual—alluring and sometimes titillating. When I was with her, I sensed an odd mix of ambiguity and androgyny, not unlike what I felt as I witnessed the hormonal transformation of Jack from his once hardened physical male self into Jocelyn, as muscle melted into a softer physical version. Gender lines blurred, throwing me off balance. I attributed my confusion to the wine and the circumstances that led to the unusual nature of our friendship. I reminded myself that Marcella was someone to hold onto, someone who might help steady me through the vertigo-filled world of change. But more than that, I was grateful to have found a true friend.

Chapter 31

The Three-Letter Word

The next few weeks were punctuated by rendezvous with Marcella—for coffee, for after class study group, for coffee, meeting up to ride to class on BART, for coffee, an evening of at-her-apartment-movie-watching, for coffee, for lunch, for coffee, and finally, the Folsom Street Fair.

"Thank you for spending all this time with me, Marcella," I said, as we walked towards the Patio Cafe in the Castro. I felt overwhelmed with gratitude towards this woman who had taken me under her wing. "You've shared so much with me; it has taught me a lot."

"You're welcome. I've enjoyed spending time with you. I'm especially glad you could come today. From the start, I've wanted you to meet some of my friends," she said with a smile. "But I knew you were concerned you wouldn't fit in, so I wanted to give you some time. Figured if you got to know me better you might be okay with meeting some harder-core dykes." She laughed when I raised my eyebrows.

"Johanna considers herself as a diesel dyke. Lois, calls herself stone butch. Labels, true, but they *are* tough cookies. To me, they're just great friends with good hearts. You will like them for who they are as people."

"I still feel awkward. Will they be okay with the fact that I'm not a lesbian?"

"I have to admit, there's a lot of prejudice in the lesbian community." Marcella answered. "But don't worry—Johanna and Lois, are cool."

"And you—what label do you wear? Until hearing these terms it would never have occurred to me to ask."

"I'm a genetic girl lesbian," Marcella answered matter-of-factly. "I was born female, identify as female, and my gender is female. But, my sexual orientation is lesbian. I'm attracted to women. I consider myself as mid-butch. All my friends know I am into the lipstick types."

"Lipstick type?" I asked.

"Like you," she confessed, her cheeks turning bright pink. "A girly-girl, that's what you are, and that's what I like."

"You're blushing!" I teased. "What would these women think of Jocelyn?"

"An MTF, or an FTM for that matter," Marcella replied, looking somewhat sheepish. "In the lesbian community they're considered bisexual."

"Not lesbian?" I stopped in surprise. "Why didn't you tell me?"

"You didn't ask," she hedged, "and besides, I wanted to get to know you better. Does it matter?" She didn't wait for my answer. "Now, let's meet my friends," she said, swinging the restaurant door wide.

Following introductions, Marcella and I sat on the bench seat, alongside a large wooden picnic table. I was quickly aware of disapproval in the eyes of the women sitting on the opposite side as they judged my sexual orientation and found it lacking. Clearly, they saw me as an outsider. I picked at my salad in silence as they talked amongst themselves and discussed the upcoming Folsom Street Fair.

"Let's go to the fair next Sunday," Marcella said loudly, as she took my hand in hers. *She must have noticed they aren't accepting me.* I felt bad for the position I had placed her in. She leaned in and whispered in my ear. "You can wear all that leather you've told me about. That's if Jocelyn doesn't care who you go with."

"Are you sure?" I asked, glancing at the group around the table. "I doubt if she'll care," I whispered back. "She's helping staff a booth for the hotline group."

"Perfect!" Marcella said, affirming her intention. "Then I'm going to pack."

"Pack?" I asked.

"Pack," she said, reaching under the table and grabbing at her crotch. "I'll wear a bulge, and a dog collar. You can lead me around on a leash." She grinned. "I'll be your *guy*."

"That will be a spectacle!" I agreed. *What the heck!* I thought.

"I can't wait!" Her enthusiasm told me that she meant every word.

"Will your friends mind my tagging along?" I needed reassurance, suspecting they would.

"I don't care what *they* think," she answered defiantly, her dark eyes flashing. "I want to share the experience with *you*."

What if I run into Jocelyn? I worried. She knew I had been spending time with a friend, but she hadn't asked, and I hadn't told her. I didn't know how to explain my own need to discover and to understand how Jocelyn's changes were going to affect me. I had come to realize that this was one of many things Jocelyn and I didn't talk about.

183

* * *

The Folsom Street Fair provided a day of boundary-crossing ambiguity. Marcella had cross-dressed convincingly as a male, bulge and all, and I was her leather-vested, corset-busted dominant in a pair of skin-clinging black leather pants I had found on sale at Wilson's. Our appearance drew enough interest that we caught the attention of several photographers who asked permission to take our photo as I led Marcella up and down Folsom Street on a leash. We had laughingly complied. I couldn't help but wonder what would happen if we ran into Joss. She hadn't been at the hotline booth when we passed. As the day went on, I tried to put Joss out of my mind and concentrate on the experience at hand.

Surrounded by the deviant social norm, Marcella and I played along. Laughing and teasing, we were on a drug- and alcohol-free high, sweating under the September afternoon sun. Finally, baked by the heat, we escaped the beer-drinking, boisterous throng of partygoers and bare-butt boys and headed back to Marcella's flat near 24th Street.

"I should go," I said, noting the time as we stepped inside her apartment.

"Cool down and have some iced tea before you go," she offered, as she helped me peel off the leather vest that clung to my sweaty back.

"Ouch! Your shoulders are burned! Here, take this," Marcella said, handing me a large bath towel. "Go in there and take a shower. Cool off. I have some aloe vera in the frig—it'll help." She opened the bathroom door, pointing out lavender and berry bath gel. "That's wonderful stuff," she said, "I think you'll like it."

The girly side of Marcella, I thought, smiling at the back and forth fluidity of self she often displayed.

"I'll fix us some iced tea," she said before closing the door behind her, leaving me standing on a soft white rug. Removing my clothes and hanging them on the door hook, I pulled the shower curtain back and stepped in. Marcella had been right. The cool water spray provided a sense of relief to my parched skin and sunburned arms and shoulders as the water ran in rivulets down my body.

I stood in the cool downpour, unaware that the bathroom door had reopened and Marcella had come back into the room. She set the tray of iced tea down on the small table that held fragrant hand soap and body lotion before shedding her clothing on the bathroom floor. Not until I heard the rustle of the shower curtain did I turn to see her entering, naked and smiling, and holding in her hand the bottle of lavender and berry liquid bath gel.

"You forgot this. Turn around and let me wash your back."

I blushed at her seeing my nakedness, and quickly turned around, at a loss for words.

I let her rub the sweet-scented gel across my shoulders and down my back, sensing her touch, keeping my eyes closed, not moving as the soap foamed and tickled its way down my back and legs.

"You're beautiful," I heard her utter. "Your figure is like the shape of a violin."

I shivered as I felt her hands caress my skin and trace the contours of my body. Her arms encircled my waist as she kissed the back of my neck, as her fingers searched for pleasure points.

"I don't know what to do," I confessed.

"It's okay," she whispered, kissing me on the mouth with cherry-flavored lips.

We stepped from the shower, and she led me to her bed.

185

"Lie with me," she said, taking me in her arms. Responding to her touch, she whispered in my ear. "I'll do to you what I'd like you to do to me. And you do to me what you would like me to do to you."

Her kisses were light but her lips felt firm. Her mouth and body were demanding, as we shared the most intimate parts of ourselves. After, lying quietly in the silence as Marcella slept, I stared at the ceiling and thought about what had just happened.

What did I feel? I felt a need to ground myself and take a hard look at who I was. Being with Marcella had been reaffirming, but curiosity had led me to her room, not sexual desire. Curiosity about how I would feel and if I could respond. For me, our interlude had been very mechanical. My sexual mind and heart had not been there. It confirmed for me that I was not a lesbian nor was I bisexual. My sexual preference was definitely male. Though I cared deeply for Marcella as a friend, I had slept with her because of my circumstances with Jack. I knew my choice would not be to seek out a lesbian sexual relationship. But *could* I be "bi-capable" with Jocelyn because of my history with Jack and the intimate relationship we had already established?

And, what about desire? I thought back to my initial attraction to Jack. I hadn't lusted after him when we met. The attraction had been his mind, his boyish humor, and his spirit of adventure. I had come to love him through knowing him. S-e-x had not been the initiating factor, but only came months later after what seemed like a normal progression of a relationship between a man and a woman. Now, after more than eight years together, we had a history of companionship and friendship, as well as a satisfying sexual and emotional relationship.

We will be entering unchartered territory as a result of our circumstances, but we have a solid foundation, I thought. But after Jack made his physical changes, how would I *really* feel? Would we be able to establish the same type of intimacy we had shared as man and woman? What we had together, could it be enough without desire?

I left Marcella's apartment that evening, feeling an overwhelming sense of clarity. She had shared her life with me for only a few weeks, but what I had learned by her sharing would stay with me for a lifetime. For that, I was truly grateful. While Marcella would always hold a very special place in my heart, I knew that without either of us expressing it, our time together had come to an end.

Chapter 32

The Missing Piece

Weeks passed and Christmas was just around the corner. Jocelyn's sex reassignment surgery was scheduled shortly thereafter, in February. Having continued her extra work search to no avail, Jocelyn was becoming more anxious than ever over what her financial future would bring. Not only did I want to keep her spirits up, but I wanted to make the holiday memorable. To that end, I hoped to mark Christmas with a special gift. *But what?* Then, it came to me.

Jocelyn had once mentioned how much she admired the black-and-white photographic art of Robert Mapplethorpe. During our phase of S&M experimentation, Jocelyn had shown me a book by Mapplethorpe in which he had documented the New York underground world of S&M.

"His photographic eye captured things many people may not have seen before and he did it with such grace and artistry. True, some of his work remains very controversial, but he is equally well-known for his photographs of celebrities, self-portraits, and even, flowers."

I had noticed a copy of *Some Women* at Acorn Books on Polk Street a few weeks before and I congratulated myself for remembering it. I recalled the book of photographs that depicted beautiful and famous women. It would be a perfect Christmas gift for Jocelyn! The next day, I drove to Acorn books. Long rows of neatly arranged books greeted me, but when I searched the "M" section, there was nothing by Mapplethorpe. My heart sank.

"Can I help you?" The balding man behind the counter asked.

"Would you have anything by Robert Mapplethorpe?" I asked. "I remember seeing a volume of *Some Women* here several weeks ago."

"Check 'Art' and 'Photography.' If you don't see it there, perhaps it's in our out-of-print section," he replied, pointing to an aisle along the right-hand wall. "If you give me a minute, I'll help you look."

As he waited on another customer, I continued my search. Finding nothing in the Art or Photography section, my disappointment peaked when I realized the out-of-print section was comprised of only two shelves. Not wanting to accept the fact that the likelihood of finding the slim, over-sized Mapplethorpe volume was unlikely, I re-perused the collection, when suddenly another title jumped out. *Conundrum.*

Could this be a copy of the book Jack had searched for years ago in the box of books from his family home . . . the same one my mom had? After many futile attempts to locate a copy in used bookstores, and failing to find it at the Antiquarian Book Faire, Jack and I had sadly concluded that this book was probably never meant to be found. I eagerly reached for the small volume, feeling grateful for the good luck. Book in hand, I opened it expectantly, while noting that the cover lacked familiarity. *Probably a reprint*, I thought to myself. I opened it randomly to page thirteen and quickly realized it wasn't the book of challenging puzzles I remembered reading as a child.

I continued to scan the text.

> "I present the confusion in cryptic terms, and I see it still as a mystery. Nobody really knows why some children, boys and girls, discover in themselves the inexpugnable belief that despite all the physical evidence, they are really of the opposite sex..."

Conundrum wasn't a children's book at all, but a book about a puzzling human condition? I examined the cover. The author was Jan Morris. *The Jan Morris?* I wondered, as I recalled the psychologist's question, "Have you heard of Jan Morris?" Bewildered, I realized that Jan Morris must be the same male-to-female transsexual!

> "A sexual purpose dominated, distracted and tormented my life: the tragic and irrational ambition, instinctively formulated but deliberately pursued, to escape from maleness into womanhood."

My hands started to shake. The connotation of what I had discovered sank in. *This has to be the book.* It was as if I had found the single, last piece of a 1,000-piece puzzle. *If only it had been in the boxes of books years ago*, I thought. I carried the book to the man at the counter.

"You found it?" he asked.

"Mapplethorpe? No," I said, handing it over. "Something better."

"Ahhh, Jan Morris. This *is* a find! You know, I heard she is doing a reading and book signing at Book Passage in Corte Madera next week." He checked a brochure lying near the cash register. "Wednesday evening. She's a fascinating person! She has written several travel books."

After paying for the book, I thanked him, and left the shop vowing that I would go to Book Passage and meet Jan Morris. *I have to; it's fate!* I thought, feeling elated. *I'll take the book and get it autographed for Jocelyn.*

* * *

I left work early Wednesday evening and drove across the Golden Gate Bridge. The small book had been placed in a plastic bag to protect it from the rain that had begun to fall. The crowded parking lot in Corte Madera told me that Jan Morris was a popular, as well as a successful writer.

Hugging the book close, I entered the store and followed signs toward the event room. It was a full house, with many people standing, eager to hear the white-haired woman who sat near the podium, wearing a tailored gray suit. She sat in a comfortable-looking chair on a raised platform behind a large table. A microphone in position, there were several travel books on display. I watched as Ms. Morris gracefully answered each question presented to her from members of the audience. I found myself studying her demeanor, but there was nothing to belie her femininity. It was hard to envision Jan Morris ever having been a male.

I was filled with mixed emotions. I found myself wishing that I had asked Jocelyn to come, even knowing that it would have prematurely exposed my surprise. But I realized she may not have come, even if invited. Recently, she had been avoiding people and was unwilling to talk about why. At this point of her transition, so close to her surgery date, I did not feel comfortable about pressing Jocelyn for a response.

Applause from the audience brought me back to the now. I watched, as row by row, people rose and formed a line with their copy of her newest book in hand. I stood quietly at the end of the line and wondered, *what will I say to this icon of male-to-female transsexuality?*

I wanted to tell her about Jack's upcoming transition to Jocelyn. I knew Ms. Morris had been married and had children before her transition. How did that work out? I wanted to ask what she thought our chances were of making it work after Jack had fully transitioned. I realized I was hoping she had answers for me. Then, it suddenly occurred to me that though other books Ms. Morris had written were brought up during the question-and-answer period, no one mentioned *Conundrum*. I strained to see her again, wondering, *is this **the same** Jan Morris? Or, had I made a mistake?*

I noticed a woman directing the line was glancing at each individual's book and receipt. Never having been at a book signing before, I wondered if without the current book and receipt in hand, I would be turned away. The thought of public rejection and humiliation made me apprehensive. Ms. Morris was taking time to speak to each individual before signing their book. *How do I explain the book is not for me, but for Jack? How much do I say? Do I tell her why?*

The line stopped and as they searched for a fresh pen. My anxiety peaked, and then won. I retreated by a side door, fled into the rain, and drove back across the Golden Gate.

The next weekend, after completing the wrapping of Christmas gifts for my kids, I retrieved the small first edition from its protective plastic bag and placed it into a red velveteen box. After tying it tight with a similar red, but silver-sparkled velveteen ribbon, I attached a card that read: "Jocelyn, In Celebration of You! All my love, Merry Christmas! Diane."

Chapter 33

Transformation Without Negotiation

Dinner was at Tommy's Wok, a local Chinese restaurant that had become one of our favorites. The person sitting across from me, however, shifting in his seat, was a man, the Jack I used to know. He looked at me with anxious eyes. When I had arrived at the Sausalito apartment that evening and the door opened, my first thought was, *where is Jocelyn?* Wearing blue jeans, T-shirt, an old loose-fitting sweatshirt and black sneakers, there was no hint of make-up, and 'her' hair had been tucked up under a man's baseball cap. For the first time in months, it was Jack standing in front of me. Now, as I sipped green tea from a tiny round white cup, I wondered, but dared not ask, *second thoughts?*

Jack nervously picked at the food with a pair of chopsticks. There was no explanation offered for his change in appearance. It was as if Jocelyn had disappeared. *What did this mean?* Tomorrow was the Big Day—Jocelyn was to leave for Portland for the sex reassignment surgery. Tonight's dinner was to be a celebration. Or, so I thought.

Had Jack begun to question his decision? I knew *I* still had questions, and concerns that Jack had never been willing to discuss with me, such as whether he had any idea what living life as a woman would really be like, socially, psychologically, emotionally. They were questions I felt were natural to ask, and ones I had tried to ask Jack early on in his process. But they were questions he had always refused to discuss, arguing that by my asking, I was not being supportive. So, eventually, I stopped asking. However, he was leaving for Portland tomorrow and I wanted to ask the questions again, even though I knew it was too late. I did not want to argue or suggest that he change his mind, I only wanted to know if he had taken the time to think everything through.

Being a woman is about more than breasts, or a vagina, or how you dress. There's the spirit and soul of a woman at her core—*do you have a vision of who that woman is? What's in your heart?* I needed to know, because Jack/Jocelyn had only said, "I want to have women friends, so that I can be all that I want to be." *What does that mean?* Jack had never told me that he felt like a woman trapped in a man's body.

Even though I continually offered to go, Jack/Jocelyn had never included me in any of his/her counseling sessions in the two years he/she had been in therapy. I had wondered, *what do they talk about? Has there been a serious discussion about the possible ramifications of the action he was about to take?* I wanted to believe there had been, but Jack never let on, and I saw no evidence of it by his comments or attitude. So much of what *he* discussed sounded superficial. My own anxiety begged the question, *what if you are making a mistake?* There was no going back. I took a deep breath, then countered my fears, and talked myself out of asking. I knew it was useless to say anything. *Wasn't his mind made up?*

I had already witnessed a shift in the dynamic of our relationship. It started with Jocelyn not doing the little things that Jack had, like opening doors, and those seemingly small, yet huge, compliments a man gives his woman—such as his look that said 'you look beautiful tonight.' Even though I felt Jocelyn was my partner, she didn't treat me in the same way that Jack had.

On the previous Sunday afternoon Jocelyn had insisted we stop at Borders on Union Square to browse for a book. Before we left, she ordered coffee and a scone. I had eaten at home and wasn't hungry. As we stood in line, she suddenly excused herself with a smile. "Diane, I'll be right back. I want to go powder my nose."

She left me alone in line. I waited for her order, paid her tab and waited at a nearby table.

Returning some minutes later, she simply said, "Thank you," without ever offering to pay and gave me the same practiced coy smile she had once demonstrated as a manipulative tool used by women on men to get what they wanted. Putting one-plus-one together, I was angry. I had never objected to paying my own way when Jack and I went out, and many times, I had offered to pay his. I never *assumed* the man would pay. But it wasn't just about going Dutch. *Was she practicing role reversal? And why was she practicing this tactic on me?* It felt more like she was assuming a sense of female entitlement and I was caught in the twilight zone of boundary-crossing ambiguity. It was further confirmation that things had changed. However, what upset me the *most*, was that I felt used.

I tried to pass it off, just as I had let other situations go in my effort to understand and adapt to the changing Jocelyn. No one expected that I would want to stay with Jack once he announced his intention to undergo sex reassignment surgery. But I had.

One friend had simply asked, "If you are heterosexual, why would you stay with Jack? Isn't that a deal breaker?" It wasn't.

What seemed to perplex people the most was how I could deal with Jack's physical exchange of an overt outward appendage for an introverted receptor. But his sexuality was not the issue. No one understood why I stayed, but I knew. We had an emotional bond—love—and I still believed that love conquered all.

I questioned if Jocelyn understood, that as she transitioned, that I was also experiencing a social, psychological and emotional transition of my own. The Portland trip was not only going to change Jack's/Jocelyn's life, it was going to change mine. *Had she ever considered how this would affect me?* I wondered. *It wasn't all about HER, was it?* All were questions I wanted to ask, but felt I couldn't. What **was** clear, was that it was transformation without negotiation. Questions unanswered would remain unanswered. Only time would tell.

Chapter 34

Fortune Smiles

"What time does your plane leave?" I asked Jack, while refilling my tiny white porcelain cup. I had wanted to accompany him to Portland for the sex reassignment surgery, but as he had done often since he had begun this very personal odyssey, he had made it clear it was something to be done alone.

"10 a.m.," the-Jack-I-knew answered, as the waitress delivered our dinner-for-two main course.

"You two seem so much in love," the waitress exclaimed, as she set the steaming plates on the table. "I have seen you here before, always in such deep conversation . . . looking into each other's eyes . . . you must love each other very much."

Jack's face reddened, as he nervously cleared his throat, and then replied, "Tommy's has great food."

"May you find happiness, and good fortune," she said with a smile, placing a small plate with two fortune cookies in the center of the table.

"Thank you," I said, thinking, *Lady Luck, do we ever need good fortune now!* I hoped that our waitress had just bestowed a good omen upon us.

"Can I at least take you to the airport?" I pressed after the waitress left.

"I have someone to take me," he answered. When I dared to ask who, the-Jack-I-no-longer-knew said, "You don't know them."

Who is this someone? I wondered.

Having either dropped off or picked up Jack/Jocelyn at the airport for every flight he/she had taken over the past eight years, this present exclusion and the secretiveness angered me. I realized that Jack/Jocelyn needed space to adjust. Therefore, I had been careful about what I said and had kept silent, all the while wanting desperately to feel included. But, by providing him/her this kind of support, I realized I constantly felt shut out.

"Portland isn't that far away, Diane," Jack reassured me. "The clinic will send a car to meet me at the airport. I will be well taken care of."

"What really bothers me is that you haven't even met the surgeon," I said. The paperwork had been completed by mail and a money order for full payment ($20,000) for the surgery had been mailed a couple of weeks earlier. All discussion with the physician had been by phone. Jack had found the surgery center and the surgeon off of the internet. Personally, I didn't feel comfortable with that.

"Check-in is by 2:00 and the surgeon will see me sometime before 4:00," said Jack-the-physician. "That's when we will have our one-on-one. We will go over my pre-op orders to see that they are in place, and then we will discuss my all-important cup size!" said the-Jack-I-knew with a broad smile. Jocelyn laughed. "Did I tell you I've decided on a C cup?"

For me, having two major surgeries in one day, breast augmentation and sex reconstructive surgery—seemed like too much.

The Chinese food sat like a rock in my stomach as I watched Jack, catch the sideways reflection of his budding torso in a wall mirror next to our table and unabashedly adjust his sweatshirt, pulling it tight over breast contours that were swollen and softened by the use of hormones. *He* had become a proud pubescent girl but without any accompanying shyness about *her* changing body.

The surgery would take about six hours. The breast augmentation would be accomplished first by placing implants. Next would be the first stage of the sex reassignment surgery. In layman's terms, the surgeon would create an opening into the pelvic cavity and invert the penile tissue into it with subsequent re-attachment of the penile tissue to the inner abdominal wall. This would create a vaginal space. The cosmetic formation of exterior female characteristics, in particular the clitoris and labia majora, would also be accomplished during this first reconstructive procedure. Further cosmetic surgery to form the labia minora would be done at a future time, after the first procedure had healed. Recovery would require a five-day stay at the clinic and another week on bed rest when Jocelyn came home. It was *major* surgery, no matter how you looked at it.

"I know you're concerned," Jack said, cracking open his fortune cookie, "but don't be. I will be fine." He read his fortune.

"Okay—I won't worry," I said without an ounce of conviction. I pulled the small piece of paper from my cookie without breaking it.

"What's yours say?" Jack asked, after reading his.

"You first," I answered.

"You won't believe it," Jack said, his smile broadening. "Listen to this: *You will do something unusual tomorrow.*"

"You've got to be kidding," I laughed, as I slowly unfolded my own tiny piece of paper and read: *An unexpected event will soon make your life more exciting.*"

"Well?" Jack prodded.

I handed the tiny paper to Jack, who smiled as he read.

"Good luck and good fortune," he said. "Our messages go together."

Chapter 35

The Way We Were

While we were having dinner, a storm blew in over the Marin headlands and brought with it a pelting rain from the west. We were grateful to have only a short ride from Tommy's Wok to the Sausalito apartment. Once parked, Jack slid quickly from the driver's seat, leaving me behind, and made a boyish sprint towards the building.

"Every woman for herself," I heard Jocelyn taunt, as Jack ran.

Feeling the force of the wind push against the car door as I attempted to exit, I realized the futility in trying to raise the umbrella I held in my hand. I struggled to adjust my coat up over my head in a makeshift effort to protect myself from the battering rain, and longed for the chivalry that came with the man who in past similar situations, had held an umbrella for us both, and kept a steady hand on the car door as I exited.

Stepping onto rain-soaked pavement, I felt water seep through the thin soles of my high heels. Without time to evaluate the best route, I began to hopscotch my way, dodging puddles formed on the uneven surface of the parking lot. As I mis-stepped into an icy sheet of water hidden by darkness, I heard Jack's unmasked voice accompanied by a peel of laughter.

"Be careful! Go to the right!" He shouted. I saw him gesture from beneath the apartment awning where he waited, safe from the downpour as I made a final leap. The rain continued its assault.

"Watch out for the drips!" Jack yelled, as cascading water fell from the sharp edge of the canvas awning. A stream of cold water had hit my head and then found its way through my wind-blown hair, over forehead and eyebrows, trickling down my cheeks, and taking my mascara with it. I gasped. Jack's laughter rang unrestrained.

For a moment, my mind flashed back to years before and how Jack had teased and laughed as I tried to navigate the shaking staircase at the apartment on Baker. *In another lifetime*, I thought, but my inner voice jumped to reassure me: *He's still the Jack you know*.

"Too late for that," I say, sidling up to him, and shaking my head doggie style, flinging wetness in his direction.

Undeterred, the-Jack-I-had-known continued to poke fun as he raced up a flight of steps to the apartment door. He examined his water-soaked Nikes and shivered from the cold before kicking the shoes from his feet, all while simultaneously putting the key in the lock. Safely inside, I handed him my drenched raincoat and watched, shivering, as he lopped it over a chair to dry.

"Here, you're dripping," he said, smiling again as he handed me a hand towel from the linen closet so that I could dry my hair. "Or, there's the blow dryer in the bathroom if you'd prefer."

As I opted for the hair dryer, Jack walked to the fireplace, squatted down and lit the logs he had carefully stacked earlier that evening. Before shedding his wet sweatshirt and pulling on a dry *Kiss of the Spider Woman* T-shirt, he slipped *Tribal Mozart* by Kazu Matsui Project into the CD player.

Several minutes later, my hair dry, I plopped down in front of the fireplace on the large eight-by-ten alpaca rug that graced the room, trying to retrieve whatever warmth I could, as the logs in the fireplace began to catch and burn. Placing my ruined high heels on the hearth, I put my wet nylon-covered feet as close to the fledgling fire as possible trying to thaw out from the cold.

"Brrrrr, it's cold! I wonder if there is snow in Portland. It *is* February," I said.

"There is," Jack said chuckling softly. "I checked the local weather report earlier today." He sat down next to me on the white cloud of softness and cuddled up close. I leaned my head on his shoulder, and listened to the familiar music playing in the background—our song.

"Diane," the-Jack-I-knew began, "with this surgery, everything will change."

I started, wondering why he had waited so long to have this conversation.

"You mean us?" I asked, suddenly defensive, and sensing my immediate apprehension around talking about all those subjects I had tried to broach, but Jack had never wanted to talk about—the intimate issues we had never discussed.

"No, actually," Jack said. "By *everything*, I mean— me."

"Jack, what? Are you questioning whether you want to go through with this? Are you having second thoughts?" I steeled myself, even more confused. Had Jack changed his mind? I held my breath, wondering what was coming next.

"No, not that," he said, gently taking my hand.

"What then, Jack? What are you trying to say?"

Jack looked at me, and then cast his eyes downward toward the floor.

"I want to be with you one last time, Diane, but I don't know if I can. The hormones . . . I have been on higher doses over the last few weeks. I might not be able to. But I want to try. Will you?" Now his eyes beseeched me.

That's it? One last time?

Now I understood tonight's charade. I didn't speak as I reached out towards Jack, the man I had always known.

There was no submission in his kiss as the warmth of the fire caressed our bare skin and we made love against a backdrop of falling rain and the snap and crackle of burning logs. He *was* the man I remembered. Our passion spent, Jack pulled the blue-and-red plaid throw, from the sofa and covered us both, before taking me into his arms and hugging me tight.

"Jack . . ." I started, as I felt my feelings begin to spill over.

"Shhhhh," he said, pulling me in even closer. "*We're* going to be okay."

As we lay in the flicker of dying firelight, I moved to give Jack a good night kiss, and saw that his face was wet with silent tears.

Chapter 36

It's a Girl!

Jocelyn had been gone for what had seemed to be a very long week, and now was back, picked up at the airport in the early afternoon and delivered home by *THEM*.

"I'll drive over this evening after work, and bring some take-out," I had volunteered. I was eager to see her, and find out the details of her trip to Portland that our way-too brief phone calls had omitted.

"Don't worry about me, I'm fine," she said with a light laugh, "but I did miss you."

"See you then," I said.

Breast augmentation and sexual reassignment surgery—new parts—how could she be fine? It was a mystery I needed to see for myself.

When I arrived, Jocelyn lay stretched out on the living room sofa. Deflated ice bags, lay on the carpet near the sofa, while others packed with cubes pressed against her chest. Her legs were elevated slightly on pillows, with another ice bag resting between her legs at the crotch. A glass of water sat on a nearby coffee table, next to a pink plastic container. Fuzzy pink slippers kicked off, lay haphazard at the end of the sofa.

"Are you warm enough?" I asked, after setting down the Chinese take-out in the kitchen. I hung my rain-soaked coat on the coat rack, shaking off the outdoor chill. The sight of the ice bags sent a shiver down my own spine. The log in the fireplace had almost died out, so without waiting for an answer, I placed another log in the fireplace and lit a match bringing welcome heat to the room. "Are you in pain?" I asked, knowing she had to be.

"I'm a bit tired, and hungry," Jocelyn answered. "Tommy's Wok?" she asked, ignoring my question about her pain.

"Of course," I answered with a smile. "Tonight's a celebration. Are you ready to eat?" I could only imagine she was on an endorphin high.

"No, not yet," said Jocelyn. "Let me show you first. You do want to see, don't you?"

Of course, I am curious, I thought. In truth, I wasn't sure I was ready to look, but I nodded, yes.

"I got my C cup," she said, slowly removing the ice bags. "I can't lift my arms up yet. I'm still too sore. Can you help?"

"Sure," I said, as I moved in quickly to take the ice.

"What do you think of the girls," she asked, exposing her fully rounded breasts.

"What do *you* think of them, is the real question," I said. "To me, they look pretty perfect. Perky is the term." I laughed, uncertain what to say.

"They *do* look perky, don't they?" Jocelyn's smile showed she was obviously pleased with the result.

"You feel okay?" I couldn't help but ask.

"Surprisingly, good."

"And the other surgery," I hesitated, "how was that?"

"See for yourself," she said, pushing away her robe, and removing the ice pack from between her legs.

I didn't know exactly what to expect, but what I saw took me by surprise. All I could think was, *you're a GIRL—anatomically correct—a FEMALE.*

"It's unbelievable. No one would know that you weren't always a female. It's amazing," was all I could say. In truth, I was stunned. Except for a bit of labial swelling, there was not a hint of an incision, a stitch, redness, or bruising.

"There's one more surgery. I go back in a year," she said, "after this has healed . . . one final cosmetic reconstruction. And those, I need to use those . . . please hand that to me," she indicated a pink plastic container.

"What is this?" I asked.

"The medical term is graduated dilators, but dildos works as well. They are used to stretch my new vagina and keep it open while it heals. I'm to use them three times a day, right now, and eventually, only once a day."

"Amazing," was all I could muster still in awe over how *far* medicine had come, and how plastic surgery could provide picture-perfect results without pain.

"What did you get at Tommy's?" Jocelyn broke the mood.

"Our favorites," I said, hopping up to retrieve napkins, plates, and chopsticks. There were walnut prawns, moo shu pork, broccoli beef, brown rice, and two cans of Coke, one a Diet for Jocelyn.

"I'm not surprised you are tired; it's been a long day," I said, dishing up the delicious fare. "Are you able to move around the apartment, or have you been lying on the sofa since you got home?" I asked, before handing Jocelyn her plate.

"I'm moving slowly, but I can get around. I should be fine by the end of this week, and next Monday I can return to work. Just no lifting," Jocelyn said, positioning herself gingerly on the sofa. "I promise to take it easy."

While I couldn't imagine her recovering so quickly, Jocelyn returned to work the next Monday, wearing her new gender and a confident smile that said, "I'm a woman."

Chapter 37

The Promise

In the months following her surgery, Jocelyn was literally a new woman. Some of it I attributed to hormonal influence, but some of it was by personal choice, as she acted on the never discussed perceptions she seemed to hold of what it meant to be a woman. I watched as the values Jack had held seemed to morph under the influence of Jocelyn's new image and her new identity took on a life of its own. It was to be expected, I told myself. After all, she *was* re-inventing herself. And with that, she had become unpredictable, as well as celibate. She wasn't *ready*, she had said. I didn't blame her. I wasn't either. But with all that had changed physically, and emotionally, I could only hope we were both still on the same page.

Jocelyn tidied up the kitchen, as I perused the *Chronicle's* pink pages and sipped down the last of my Sunday morning coffee.

"Jocelyn, the Harvest Festival is next weekend!" I exclaimed, spotting the ad. I always looked forward to going to the event, and couldn't help but think that it represented something from our past together that had not changed.

The Harvest Festival was the one winter event that we had not missed in nine years. I remembered how in years past Jack and I had talked about wanting to go on the first day, but our work always prevented it. Jocelyn's diminishing clientele had opened up days in her schedule. Maybe this year we could go on the first day and beat the traffic?

"I'm pretty sure that I can get the day off, if you want to go on Friday," I suggested, still thinking about the limited edition Klimt. I had wanted the watercolor-on-silk wall art, *The Kiss*, ever since I saw it in the artist's photos. Last year, intent on buying it, we had gone to the festival on Sunday but had lost out to a buyer on Saturday. The artist had promised she would bring another 'next year'. This could be our chance. "We could get *The Kiss* if we go Friday," I added.

"I can't go until Sunday!" Jocelyn shouted back from the kitchen. "I've got too much work at the office. To my surprise, I'm already booked into late Friday, and with the office paperwork to get out, I expect I will have to work Saturday to complete it."

"Then, Sunday it is. That works for me!" I said, masking my disappointment as I thought about the artist's print. *No matter what, we'll enjoy it*, I vowed, and I tossed both the newspaper and my unhappiness aside.

Realizing the time, I picked up my jacket from the window seat as Jocelyn came out of the kitchen, drying a juice glass with a hand towel.

"I have to go," I said, "I have things to do with the kids today."

"I'll see you at work, tomorrow, then." Jocelyn replied. "And next Sunday—we'll go, I promise." Then, she hugged me tight.

The week passed quickly and Jocelyn's work seemed to consume all of her time. There hadn't been

212

much chance to discuss the Harvest Festival outing because our usual meet-up for lunch had been interrupted by 'the patient comes first.' As she had predicted, the weekend, began with Jocelyn's playing catch up with office work. I began to wonder if busier-than-usual-Jocelyn was feeling anxious about going to the event and that she might be in avoidance pattern. Much of our enjoyment in attending past festivals was to see certain vendors that had become old friends. No longer Jack, Jocelyn had learned over the past few months that many of those who had known her before her transition had given her mixed reactions. In short, we had come to learn that not everyone was accepting. *It will be a test in courage*, I thought, remembering her promise to go.

Chapter 38

It's All in the Cards

I awoke Sunday morning looking forward to the day.

"Mom! My appointment is this morning! You remembered, didn't you?" Kristie's voice sounded an alarm, as I dished up scrambled eggs to a plate of hash browns and bacon.

"It's today?" I had clearly forgotten.

"You can still go, can't you? I made an appointment for eleven o'clock. You can take me before you go to the Harvest Festival with Joss."

A senior class project on dreams required Kristie to investigate three different theories around the meaning of dreams. She had read scientific journals and understood how the conscious and subconscious state of mind affected one's dreams. She had attended a New Age class on lucid dreaming and analyzed how one can affect their own dream state. However, her final assignment was to speak to an expert regarding dream interpretation. The closest she could find was a woman named Mary, who had good referrals from Psychic Eye, a New Age shop on Fell Street. Mary provided dream interpretation through use of the tarot. Kristie had made an appointment with Mary to have a persistent dream interpreted that she had been having over a number of years.

I called Jocelyn, and when she did not pick up, I left a message on her answering machine. "I'll be ready to go at one thirty, after I run an errand with Kristie. Pick me up at home?" And, off we went to consult with soothsayer Mary and her tarot cards.

Entering the incense-filled shop on Fell Street, we were pointed to a small curtained cubicle at the back of the shop. A rose-colored glow emanated through the opening in the curtain wall. Through it, I glimpsed a pretty, young woman in her late twenties sitting in a meditative state. I had expected an old crone, shawl covered, gray-haired, and snaggle-toothed. I wondered about the ability, or experience, of someone so young, and lost faith.

Pulling the curtain back, the young woman invited the student and her skeptical mother into the small room. We all sat at a small table.

"What brings you to me?" The young woman asked Kristie.

"I'm doing a class assignment on dreams. I was told that you are able to interpret dreams through the use of the tarot."

The young woman nodded as she picked up the deck of cards.

"I want you to formulate a question in your mind you have about your dream. What is it you would like to know? Do not tell me what your question is," she warned, as she deftly mixed and shuffled the cards.

"Do you have your question in mind?"

"Yes, I do," said Kristie, thinking about a boy who had promised he would love her forever, and then had just seemed to disappear from her life.

"Using your left hand, please chose a card," instructed the seer after she lay ten cards face down on the table. Next, one-by-one, she upturned each card. "Though he went away, he has not forgotten you," said Mary, with a quick glance at the upturned card.

Kristie took a deep breath and seemed to relax.

"He will marry," added Mary, turning another card.

"Me?" Kristie asked, leaning on her every word.

"No," said Mary. "Another."

Kristie's face fell.

"He will marry first—you will find your happiness and marry many years later."

Kristie's eyes grew wide." Marry . . . who? Who will I marry in many years . . .?"

"The cards do not reveal anymore," Mary said, scooping the cards from the table, indicating the reading was over. "I hope I answered your question."

A surprised Kristie thanked her and handed her twenty-five dollars in cash.

"Yes, you did," Kristie said sadly, "but now I am left with other questions—about the future."

The young woman smiled. "I have found the cards are seldom wrong."

"Would you like me to read your cards?" asked the young woman with a casual look towards me.

"Thanks, but I'm okay," I said.

"Oh, mom, come on!" Kristie encouraged. "Ask a question."

The young woman continued to shuffle the cards.

"We are here. Sure! Why not? I'll take the challenge. I'm curious about what the cards might say."

"Think of your question," repeated the young woman.

I closed my eyes and thought hard. All I wanted to know was whether things would work out between Jocelyn and myself. I posed the mental question.

Unlike the card pattern she drew for Kristie, this time, the visionary drew the cards, one-by-one, and placed them in a six-card formation. She turned the cards over, slowly studying each, her face showing a growing concern.

"I'm sorry, I cannot read your cards," she said, suddenly pushing back from the table.

"What? Why?" I questioned, confused and feeling cheated by her sudden inability.

Mary's countenance had gone from relaxed and serene to furrowed bewilderment.

"I am not sure how to interpret what I see. Something is wrong. I'm not seeing clearly," she said, starting to stand, but leaving the cards lay.

"No wait! Please. Can't you just tell me what you see?" My curiosity was now peaked and my question needed an answer even more than ever.

"Very well," she pointed. "This card represents you. And this card, sliding her finger down the line of cards, is also a woman. She represents darkness. She is not your friend." She took a deep breath. "My puzzle is in this card. At first, I saw a man, but no, not a man . . . a woman—now I cannot tell. I cannot differentiate. I do not understand what this means. Something is wrong," she said, and then she quickly scooped up the cards. "I don't know what you have planned for today, but you should abandon your plan. It will bring you nothing but pain."

She moved quickly to draw aside the room's curtain, in a final signal of her frustration. "I'm sorry I could not answer your question. There is no charge," The young woman said, as she saw me reach into my purse.

We got up, thanked her, and with unsettled feelings, left the shop.

"I am not sure what to think of all that." I said to Kristie once we were outside and the sounds of Fell

Street traffic brought us back to reality. "Did she answer your questions about your dream?"

"Time will tell. I just hope I stop having the dream!"

"Do you want to talk about it?" I asked.

"Not yet," Kristie smiled. "I'm going to wait and see what happens."

"Okay," I said, returning her smile.

"What about you, Mom? What she said . . . it was kind of crazy, but it made some weird sense, didn't it?"

"It was interesting Mary's cards saw a man that was a woman! I think it scared her. She didn't know how to interpret the information, but how can I blame her? Who would?" I said. I thought of the all-knowing eight-ball I owned as a kid, remembering the simple yes or no answer, and wondering how Mary could have seen what she did. "She almost made me a believer, Kristie," I laughed. "But like you said, time will tell."

When we got to the car, my cell phone showed I had a message. I listened.

"Jocelyn left a message," I told Kristie. "She's sorry but work has taken over her day. She can't go to the Harvest Festival after all, and she says she'll call me later tonight. It's a bummer, this will be the first time we'll have missed in nine years."

"Let's go, Mom!" Kristie offered. "I'll go with you. I know how you wanted to go! It'll be fun."

I didn't hesitate. "Let's do it! It'll be a mother-daughter day!"

* * *

The festival wasn't much different than past years. As we walked through the vendor stalls, I searched for the old friends, saying hello to some, missing others. As I suspected, the Klimt painting, *The Kiss*, was gone. "I sold my last one just over an hour ago," the artist lamented. Kristie, however, found a silver ring, purchased it, and happily donned it on her pinky finger.

"Want to get something to eat Kristie? I'm hungry."

The morning's activity, along with the day's disappointments, had begun to wear on me. *The cards were right*, I thought. *Jocelyn couldn't come to the festival. It does hurt.*

As my eyes searched the crowd for the best food vendor, I stopped short and grabbed at Kristie's arm.

"Tell me I'm not seeing who I'm seeing!"

"Where?" Kristie looked around searching the crowd.

"There!" I tried to control my voice and not scream out in anger. I was back in the hallway the day Jack had told me he thought he was HIV positive. There was confusion, disbelief, and a sense of overwhelming betrayal. An anger for which there were no words.

"It's Jocelyn . . . and she's with Marta!" I said.

"Calm down, Mom! Don't give her the satisfaction of seeing you're angry," Kristie implored.

I started to approach them, but stopped. I didn't know what I would say. Jocelyn hadn't seen me but, Marta had. The dominant was no longer in control. She grasped and pulled at Jocelyn's arm.

"Come on, let's go." I saw her mouth speak inaudible words over the noise of the crowd. Jocelyn followed the direction of Marta's gaze and turned. Seeing me, she froze. The would-be-dominant stood quaking behind her.

"Stay here," Jocelyn mouthed back. Then she moved through the crowd towards me.

"Come on," I said to Kristie, "I don't want to talk to her. Let's leave."

Chapter 39

Excuses, Excuses

Jocelyn broke through the festival crowd and caught up with us. I turned and faced her. "I didn't tell you, because I knew you would be upset."

"You're right, I am. But this isn't the time or place to discuss it." I was at my boiling point and I could feel Kristie's hand on my arm.

"I'll go drop Marta off, and come pick you up. If you haven't eaten, we can go get dinner and talk. I'll be there in less than an hour. I'll explain everything."

I didn't answer, but stormed out of the Concourse Pavilion, with Kristie leading the way.

"What was that about?" asked Kristie. As angry as I was, she slid into the car next to me.

"I don't know," I answered, my voice and hands shaking, wondering what Jocelyn's excuse would be this time.

As far as I knew, Jocelyn had been true to her word and had had no contact with Marta since the Exotic Erotic Ball almost two years before. There had been nothing to indicate otherwise, and I had been watchful. Forgive, but don't forget had been my motto. *So, what was going on?*

"They both acted afraid when they saw us," the always-observant Kristie pointed out.

"That wasn't lost on me," I said.

Jocelyn arrived within fifteen minutes of my own arrival home. She called and I met her at the curb.

"Let's go to Mel's," Jocelyn said. It had become our new go-to-place when we went out—a place both of us could afford.

We rode in silence. *I'm going to let her do the talking*, I told myself, not wanting to put any words in her mouth. Meanwhile, I could hardly bring myself to look at her.

"Start talking," I said, after we had ordered a burger and fries.

"It's not what you might be thinking," Jocelyn started. "Marta called *me*. She's in a fix."

"What do you mean?" I said, feeling no compassion.

"She heard through the grapevine I might be looking for a roommate."

"What do you mean by that," I asked, clearly taken aback. "You haven't mentioned needing a roommate. We're planning to move by next summer anyway—perhaps somewhere else. That's only six months from now. So why would you make a change now?"

"I need to move. I can't afford the Sausalito apartment any longer. I didn't say anything to you because I didn't want to worry you. But, I have been looking around for something cheaper. There's not much out there that I can afford. The only thing I found is in the East Bay, and it's not a neighborhood I'm really comfortable in. Even then, I need a roommate to help meet expenses. Six months, that's all. I know you aren't ready to move yet, so I'm looking at alternatives until then. It just so happens that Marta unexpectedly lost her city apartment, needs a place, and was looking for a roommate, too."

I wondered, *was Marta using her dominatrix-influence to manipulate Jocelyn?* She had shown a **significant** hold on Jack in the past and I had heard of Subs supporting their Dom's through cash gifts. *Was this a way for her to wile her way back into Jocelyn's life? Do I dare even suggest this possibility?* I pushed the thought to the back of my mind. *Jocelyn has to be smarter than that!* What I had noticed was that since Jack became Jocelyn, she was a lot more susceptible to the influence of others—particularly women. I saw it as Jocelyn's effort to make women friends. *She has a lot to learn, I thought.*

"I finished up at the office earlier than expected and gave her a call," Jocelyn continued. "Knowing the festival would end in a couple of hours, I thought I'd take care of two things at once. There was something I wanted to get for you."

Get for me? How clever, I thought, feeling manipulated. *How can I be angry if Jocelyn's doing it for me!"*

"What were you going to get for me?" I questioned, looking her in the eye.

"I can't tell you, or it won't be a surprise," Jocelyn answered, frustrated and getting back on point. "I figured Marta and I could walk and talk, and I wouldn't miss the festival. This could be a solution for both of us, but I told her I needed to talk to you before I could commit to anything."

"Why couldn't you have just told me, Jocelyn?"

"Because I didn't want to upset you until I'd had a chance to discuss it with her, and come to some conclusion for myself."

"You mean you are actually considering this?"

"It would just be for six months," Jocelyn concluded.

"So, you *have* decided."

"Yes, I think it would be best," she said.

"After everything that happened around her before—what about us? It's going to be awkward considering how I feel about Marta."

"Six months, Diane, that's all. The expenses of transition have drained my reserves and I don't want to touch the funds I set aside for an eventual home. My patient load is up and down and if my finances don't improve, I need to seriously look outside the Bay Area for work. Just as we've discussed, it might be best to relocate to some place where no one knew me before. Start over, start fresh, someplace more affordable."

"Only six months—I can be ready to move by then," I affirmed.

"It's okay then?"

"If there is no other way. Do I have a choice?"

"I'm going to call back the person in Berkeley. It's a small house and the price is right. The commute will be longer, but I can arrange my schedule so I don't have to cross the bridge every day. It'll be a good way to save some dollars. I'll let Marta know we've talked. The sooner I move, the better."

As I swallowed the last bite of my hamburger, and swigged down my Coke, I wondered, *what would the cards have to say about this?*

Chapter 40

On the Outside Looking In

"It's only a couple of blocks off of Ashby," Jocelyn enunciated in her well-practiced voice. "It's not hard to find," she said, handing me the address she had written on a small slip of paper.

It had only taken a couple of days for Jocelyn to finalize the new rental and move. "I'll get a truck and pick up a couple of day laborers to load it."

Jack had asked for my sons' help in two previous moves, but not this time. This made logical sense. The oldest boys were away at school, and the younger two, though respectful toward Jocelyn, had not fully adjusted to the idea of *her*. *Give them time*, I thought. Jocelyn's not asking proved to me she understood without me having to say anything.

* * *

Ashby was familiar to me from the many weekend trips we had made to Berkeley over the years to scour bookstores along Telegraph Avenue. Avoid car-wrecking potholes, I made my way to Sacramento Street and turned right, my eyes looking for a cross street that would lead to Jocelyn's new residence. The neighborhood was a far cry from prestigious Pacific Heights or up-scale Sausalito. I understood why

Jocelyn did not want me to see it before now. She worried I would think it was below the standard she had always set for herself, and in her new persona, she knew I worried about her safety even more. But was she truly this desperate?

I made a left, passing a vacant corner lot enclosed by a wire fence topped with barbwire that predominantly displayed a large yellow billboard. The lot was dotted with discarded sofas, chairs, and other household items that had been randomly dumped. I took another look at the address Jocelyn had scrawled for me on a tiny scrap of paper, before stopping alongside a broken curb in front of a small, white, one-story house with barred windows.

Two small children played in the weed-infested yard of a run-down house next door, and a tall, lean, but muscular, teenaged boy in baggy pants, wearing a Rastafarian print T-shirt, knelt on the cracked concrete driveway, working to replace a flat tire on a bicycle, while a tired-looking large-breed dog sunned himself nearby.

Several broken-down cars and trucks lined the tree-sparse street. Sliding out of my newly-washed and polished, bright red Jeep, I double-checked the locked car door before crossing the closely cropped lawn towards the front steps of Jocelyn's new home. Through the metal bars, I could see crisp, white gossamer curtains had been hung at the front window, a shade was half-pulled. I pressed the doorbell and heard a "buzz" echo somewhere inside.

Instantaneously, the door opened. Had she been watching for my arrival? Pushing the screen door open, her greeting was an unsmiling, nervous, furtive glance.

"Hi!" I said smiling, then stepped back in surprise as she quickly slid through the screened doorway, leaving it to close with a bang. She moved past me towards my car, leaving me to trail behind.

"I was hoping to see your new place," I said, stating the obvious. Jocelyn had reached my car and was already gripping on the door handle.

"Let's go," she said in a brusque manner. "I have to be back soon."

I was confused. *Hadn't she called and asked if I wanted to drive over from San Francisco to see the house she was renting?* It had been her idea to go for a late lunch, so we could talk about new job prospects and our move next summer.

"I don't know Berkeley," I said, as I slid behind the wheel and I turned the key. Inwardly, I was beginning to bristle with irritation.

"So where were you thinking of going for lunch?"

"Let's just drive, Diane, I know of a place and we can sit and talk. Start by making a right at the corner."

I followed Jocelyn's direction and turned on University Avenue. We headed west until we entered East Shore State Park.

"I found this place just last week," Jocelyn said, motioning that I should turn into a parking lot that bordered a boat-filled marina. "Let's park here."

"I don't see a restaurant," I said.

Jocelyn turned and sat with her back to the passenger door, and adjusted her large handbag across her chest as if it were a shield.

"I did want you to come today and see the place. I was looking forward to it, but at the last minute, Marta had the day off, and stayed home."

"So, I'm not going to see your place?" *Why would it matter if Marta was there or not?* I wondered.

"Not today."

"You pulled me all the way over here from San Francisco to tell me this?"

"I know, I'm sorry. I did want to see you. I didn't want to just talk on the phone, because with Marta there, now I don't have much privacy."

"So, what's going on?" I asked, trying to quell my irritation.

"I've a possible job opportunity. Do you remember the hospital I told you about down near L.A.? They got back to me yesterday and they want an interview."

"Santa Clarita? Jocelyn, that's great!" I said, letting go of some of my uneasiness.

"I can't go during the week, so they suggested next Saturday afternoon. I thought we might drive down, if you are willing. After the interview, we can drive around the area, see if we like it, maybe even look at an apartment or two. It will give us a chance to get an idea about the possibilities."

I breathed a sigh of relief at her inclusion.

"Do you mind driving?" Jocelyn asked. "I can pay for the gas."

I wasn't looking forward to the long drive, but thought, *it will give us time together.*

"Yes, I'm game," I agreed.

"Okay then, I'll give the director a call and confirm the time," she said glancing at her watch. "I've got to get back," she said, as she fidgeted with her purse.

"So soon?" My stomach reminded me it was closer to dinner than to lunch.

"I have to get back; Marta's waiting for me," Jocelyn said. "We need to go to the grocery store."

Pulling up to the small, window-barred house, I held onto the positive thoughts of moving away and starting over. Of leaving the negatives of the past couple of years behind us—including Marta.

"Another thing, I almost forgot," added Jocelyn, exiting the car and turning back to talk to me through the open window. "I discontinued seeing my regular therapist. She was too expensive. I've started seeing another counselor within the LGBT community. I've only seen her a couple of times but I'd like us to go together and talk to her. You know, about what I've been going through."

What WE have been going through, I thought, surprised she wanted me to speak with her therapist after all of this time. "Sure," I nodded.

"Okay, good. I'll make an appointment when we get back."

I couldn't help but think, *with everything we have going on, why now?*

Chapter 41

The Mirage

I-5 is a miserable freeway to travel if you've driven it more than a few times before. This was to be our third trip in five weeks. The only thing it had going for it was that it was the most direct route to our destination.

"I'll take a book," Jocelyn said, and she did. As I drove, that gave me time to think.

Jocelyn's initial interview had gone well, taking only a couple of hours with the hospital's director. At the end of the interview, she had disclosed her transitional status to the director, but had asked for confidentiality when it came to the remainder of the staff. "I'm beginning anew," she confessed. "I just want everyone to get to know me as *me*." She hoped that the director would honor her request, but wondered if it would affect his decision to hire her.

The following Monday, the director's invitation to come back for a second interview with department heads and nursing staff allayed Jocelyn's fears and added to her confidence. The second trip to interview resulted in "How soon can you start?"

The future promised the new start for which we had been hoping for. All we needed to do was to find a place to live, and get my resume to local recruiters. Hence, the reason for trip number three.

"Let's take a look at the apartment complex around the corner from the hospital first," Jocelyn said, looking up from her to-do list. "A rental is still an option, but, I want to check in with the realtor I spoke to yesterday. She has a house for sale out of town that sounded interesting. It even has fruit trees." she said, as she appearing to ponder plucking plums from a tree. "I'd like that."

"A house with fruit trees? I thought we decided as little upkeep as possible—no yard work," I reminded her. "With your schedule, and my daytime work, who will do it?"

"I don't know, but it's worth a look," she answered, ending the conversation as she closed her notebook, put on her reading glasses, and began to peruse the *Wall Street Journal*.

A house, outside of town, I thought. *Last week she was adamant it would be an apartment rental close to the hospital. What caused the change in mind? What happens if Santa Clarita doesn't work out?* Predictable Jack had become unpredictable Jocelyn. *Get used to it!* I laughed to myself. *I'm sure this won't be the last surprise.*

The highway stretched to the horizon and I noticed a sign for Los Banos, forty-three miles ahead. I made a mental note to turn off at Highway 152 and head for the Dairy Queen. *Los Banos can be a pit stop and we can get an ice cream cone—something to break the monotony*, I decided.

My eyes scanned the valley to my left. There were fields, cows, and an occasional windmill and the California aqueduct that paralleled I-5. To my right, hills empty fenced fields. *Wait! Is that an ostrich standing at the fence next to the freeway? How could that be?* I wondered. There was nothing else around for miles.

"Jocelyn, look!"

"What?" she said glancing straight ahead.

"There, in the field," I said, pointing to the right, as we passed by. "Turn around, look! It's an ostrich, of all things!"

Jocelyn turned, and wiggled her way around to look back, pulling off her reading glasses. "Can't see a thing with these on," she complained, straining to look back at the field disappearing behind us. "I see something, but I can't make it out. You think you saw an ostrich? Why would an ostrich be out here?"

"I don't know, I was wondering the same thing—but I did see it!"

"I believe you," Jocelyn said, as she smiled her 'there, there' smile and settled back with her newspaper.

I pondered the questions, *who, what, where, and why* for the next thirty-five miles, vowing to look for it on our return trip, and ultimately wondering, *was I seeing things? Very bizarre*, I thought. *What did it mean?*

Chapter 42

Can't See the Forest for the Trees

Looking back, I was amazed at how everything was falling into place, and coming together better than we could have ever planned. It was going to be a fresh start, and it felt good. I felt good.

"I've decided on the two-story country home. It's too good to be true, something I can't pass up!" Jocelyn sprung her announcement on me as I entered her office. "I called and made an offer."

We had discussed that with her new job, banked cash from the sale of her San Francisco home, and my promising job prospects, it was definitely affordable. We would be buying our first home.

"Not only that, I'll be starting my new position on the thirtieth of next month, seven weeks from today," Jocelyn said with a smile, as she walked around her desk and counted off the days on her office wall calendar. "They're being gracious—they needed someone yesterday. They know how hard it is to relocate. And that, I'm grateful."

"That's great," I said, feeling their graciousness was much more than that. It was a sign of respect, and more than just gratitude, Jocelyn was happy.

I was happy too. I had begun my own process of clearing and packing. My sons were making their own way now, college, jobs, and their own apartments. Their childhood treasures had been packed away for safekeeping. Kristie would leave for college soon, and we had been shopping for needed dorm items. The kids were leaving the nest, and off on new adventures and so was I.

I hadn't told Jocelyn that one of the recruiters I had contacted on one of our previous trips, had called me with a job prospect. With Kristie's help, I had made trip number four the day before, to do a job interview. It had been a 2:30 a.m. start for a 10 a.m. interview, but we made it. It had gone so well, I gave Kristie a high-five when I got back to the car for the return trip. All I had to do now was cross my fingers.

I held onto my own news. *Way too much going on.* I decided, *I'll tell Jocelyn when I know something.* I was glad I could provide a new employer with a start date.

"By the way," Jocelyn's voice worked its way into my consciousness, "I've been so busy the past few weeks, I've put our going to the therapist off—but I made that appointment we talked about. It's for day after tomorrow, is that okay with you?"

In truth, I had forgotten all about it. "Of course," I said, wondering if Jocelyn would feel the need to continue seeing a therapist once we moved.

Chapter 43

Out of the Frying Pan, Into the Fire

Taking time off from work, I drove myself to Jocelyn's therapist's office, which was located on a quiet residential street off of Geary Boulevard in the Richmond District. I understood it to be an introductory session, primarily, to say hello. But it opened up the opportunity to express my feelings for Jocelyn and to tell my side of our story, to express some of the difficulties I initially had with her transition, and examine where I was in my feelings and thoughts now.

"It was very hard at first," I said to the therapist, as the session started. "I didn't know what to think. I didn't understand it at all. Jocelyn wasn't helpful, and I realized that I would have to seek out information and help to understand for myself, which I did," I said, with a sideways look at Jocelyn.

Jocelyn looked straight ahead and didn't acknowledge or deny any of what I said.

"You say Jocelyn made no effort to help you understand," asked the auburn-haired therapist, "Do you know why?"

"Not really. I was surprised at her attitude. By that time, we'd been together as a couple for over seven years. I thought I knew her pretty well, Jack, that is. I wanted to talk about it, but he seemed unwilling to share his thoughts, always saying 'You wouldn't understand.' He—rather, *she*—didn't like me asking any questions. Jack seemed to feel that by asking questions I was not being supportive. Sorry," I said, looking at Jocelyn. "When I think about the past, Jocelyn's duplicity is still strong in my memory."

The therapist nodded as if she understood and asked, "How did you feel about Jack—Jocelyn's unwillingness to share with you?"

"At first, it hurt a lot," I confessed. "I felt rejected, like he—*she*—was pushing me away."

"So, you sought out information on your own?"

"Yes."

"And now, what are your thoughts?"

"We've gone through a lot. I loved Jack and we had a lot in common. Since Jack's transition, my feelings haven't changed. I have the same feelings for Jocelyn. And, to answer your initial question, I realize now how hard it must have been for Jack to tell me his secret—to come out. I assume he thought I would leave him, because I wouldn't be able to accept his transition," I said, before adding, "He underestimated my love."

"And Jocelyn, what are you thinking and feeling as you listen to what Diane is saying?"

Jocelyn shifted sideways in her chair, crossed, and uncrossed her legs, adjusted her long skirt, picked up her can of soda from the table, and played with the straw.

"Someone else wants to go with me," Jocelyn blurted out, not meeting my unbelieving eyes.

"What do you mean, someone else wants to go with you?" My voice shouted in a knee jerk reaction. "Who? You said no, didn't you?" Then I laughed, thinking it must be a joke.

The silence was almost deafening before Jocelyn's voice squeaked, "Marta."

I looked at the therapist in disbelief. *Help me out here!* My mind shouted.

"Marta!" I retorted. "What is she thinking? Why would she think you'd leave me and go away with her?"

But the only voice I could hear was the one in my head. *Haven't we been together now over ten years? Who has stood by you through everything? Who has driven you back and forth to job interviews? Didn't we recently decide where we wanted to live—together? Aren't we buying a house together? You've supported my job search effort; you know I have upended my life. I am packing. My children have grown and gone their way. I am alone now, ready to go with you like we have planned. This can't be happening.*

"Marta?" As I repeated her name, I felt my head begin to buzz, and the room swirled as I struggled for air. *Calm down,* I thought to myself. *Marta's manipulating Jocelyn.* That was all that my mind could conclude.

"Yes," Jocylen squeaked again.

After everything we've gone through? I thought. *After struggling with the life issues of your changes? After four years of surreal mind warp, moving forward day-by-day, working to conquer fears brought on by your new life? After I held you close, accepting your new self along with all of the unknowns, after sleeping together as one? After all of this, there is someone else? Marta?*

I finally found my voice. "Marta? Are you saying you want *her* to go with you?"

Jocelyn looked uneasy and studied the soda can she held. No explanation followed; none was intended.

"Jocelyn, you're waffling again," said the therapist. "You asked Diane here today to talk to her. She has

239

been forthright with her feelings and asked you a reasonable question. Will you answer her?"

I suddenly turned on the therapist, feeling coerced.

"Did you know *this* is why Jocelyn asked me to come here today?"

"Jocelyn asked only that we begin a conversation. Jocelyn?" She asked.

Jocelyn remained mute.

"Diane," the supportive voice of the therapist stopped my thought train as it raced down a track to nowhere. "Before you came in today, Jocelyn had also suggested that at some point the three of you might want to meet to talk. Jocelyn, please let us know if this is not the case."

"The *three* of us?" I interrupted, wondering if I had heard right.

"Yes. Jocelyn, Marta and yourself," said the therapist. "I would be here of course, and help lead the discussion."

I looked at Jocelyn, who continued to shift in her seat but did not answer, so I took it upon myself to answer for us both.

"If that is what it takes to find out what is going on, then hell yeah!" I said. "When?"

"I have an opening tomorrow afternoon; would that work for all of you?"

Without waiting to hear Jocelyn's response, I agreed, got up, and left the therapist's office, leaving Jocelyn behind. As I headed for my car, I remembered the ostrich standing in the open field along I-5 and realized, perhaps it *had* been a sign, for me to get my head out of the sand.

Chapter 44

Ménage à Trois

The time had come to confront the elephant in the room.   Jocelyn had encouraged me to speak to her therapist. She had made statements about what Marta wanted, but she had not voiced outright that Marta's demands were also her own. Or, had she? I was angry and upset, but read in her behavior that something was off.   Considering all that we had planned over time together, all that we had been through the past four years during her transition, and our last weeks of planning to move, what I needed to understand was what was behind all this and why was Jocelyn making the choices she was making? None of it made sense. I took a step back, tried to control my emotion, and get a grip. *What was going on?* Not trusting Marta, I wondered, *what type of power trip is Marta on? What does Jocelyn really want?* And, most importantly, *what should I do?*

Jocelyn had sunk into the large over-stuffed chair at the end of the room, her tall, thin frame engulfed within its lavender-hued floral print. I sat stiffly on the small loveseat across from Marta, who was dressed in a loose-fitting orange-colored sweat suit.   Plus-sized, Marta sat slouched with legs crossed on an over-stuffed settee. *She can't hurt you*, I thought to myself. *Be strong.* Marta glared in my direction and I gave her back a cool 'eat shit' look, and with it gave myself a sense of power.

As the therapist entered, Jocelyn smiled a hello. I gave a tense nod of my head and Marta smirked. I wondered what I was in for. It no longer felt like a therapy session.   The sense of power I had felt moments before began to subside and began to be replaced by a feeling that I was about to run a gauntlet. Marta shifted in her seat and I noticed coffee stains on the front of her orange sweatshirt and my own sense of *it's going to be okay* surged. Again, I wondered, *what attracted Jocelyn to this woman?*

As we waited for the therapist to begin, Marta, pulled out a chain at her throat and exposed a marcasite pendant, dangling it like the proverbial carrot.

And I took the bait.

"Where did you get that necklace?" It was my voice shouting at the woman in orange, but I already knew the answer.

Glancing at Jocelyn, I saw a look of dismay cross her face. The therapist was taken aback.

"I have one just like it!" I said, remembering the sparkling stone-encrusted case that had attracted my eye years ago on one of our Sunday afternoon explorations of The Museum Company. Jack had later surprised me with the pendant as a birthday gift. Tears welled up, as I recalled how special the necklace had been to me—and how I had always treasured his gift. The woman in orange scrutinized it as it hung on its silver chain.

"I don't know why you are getting so upset. It's just a bauble," Marta said, as she calmly slipped it back into her sweatshirt. "Jocelyn gave it to me for my birthday four years ago."

"*Your* birthday?   Four years ago?"   It was information I quickly absorbed.

"It was the first gift Jocelyn ever gave me.   Four years ago, wasn't it?"   She said with a smile at Jocelyn.

Jocelyn was still not forthcoming as if the chair had swallowed her up.

"Four years!"   I repeated it aloud only once, but the words kept echoing in my ears.

"We've been together for four years.   Jack wasn't the only one.   Pardon, Jocelyn isn't the only one.   We have an open arrangement.   I have five male partners, all subs—Jocelyn is my *female* partner."   Marta's mouth just kept moving.

I sat frozen.   My ears tuned in on every word, but it was her final comment that sent me over the edge.

"Sex has been great!   I told him early on you wouldn't be okay with it.   Most women don't go for polyamory.   But, don't worry, I've known about you forever.   I try to be careful.   I don't think you have to worry about catching anything."

"What?"   I looked at Jocelyn in disbelief, hearing only the word 's-e-x'.   "Is she telling the truth?   You have been having a sexual relationship with her, *and* with ME?"

Jocelyn's silence screamed her answer.

I was battling to retain what was left of my dignity.   I felt like I had been played by Tweedledee and Tweedledum.   Marta read my face.

"Jocelyn, can't you feel her pain?   Have some compassion," Marta chided, as she continued the game.

The heat of my anger had dried the tears.   I stood and walked across the room as Jocelyn sank deeper into the chair.

"How could you?"   I screamed in a whisper.   "Stand up!   STAND UP!"

243

As she rose slowly from the chair, I slapped her with all of the force I could muster, knocking her back. No one moved.

It's over, done, finished, I said to myself. *There is no going back.*

Holding my head high, I let myself out and walked two blocks to my car. I got in, and only then, gave myself permission to drown in my own tears.

Chapter 45

The Head of Holofernes

"Is it really you?" the Instant Message asked.

I took a moment to reply. While checking an old e-mail address, I had accidentally opened the IM tab.

It has been over four years, I thought.

"Diane?" Another line of type flashed on the screen.

I hesitated a few more seconds before clicking out, "Jocelyn?"

"It's me. How are you?"

Four years, I thought again.

I could type faster than most people could talk, but my fingers sat motionless on the keyboard as moments passed.

"Are you still there?" another line of type flashed.

"Yes," I finally replied into the box at the top of my screen.

"I tried to see you before I moved to Santa Clarita. I went to your place. I knocked, but you weren't home. I left your gift. Did you get it?"

It's been over four years . . .

Gift? I stared at the typed message on the screen, and remembered the Sunday afternoon just before Jocelyn's anticipated move to Southern California. I had returned home to find a package wrapped in butcher paper sitting on my doorstep. "Klimt Silkscreen Art" a small label read in the upper right-hand corner. A small card was taped just beneath it. My breath had caught when I saw it. I had not had any contact with Jocelyn since the afternoon at the therapist's office. So much had happened in the months since the Harvest Festival, that I hadn't given Jocelyn's comment about getting me something at the festival another thought. Seeing the package, my breath caught as I had wondered, *is this Jocelyn's way to try to make amends?*

I had taken the package inside and anxiously read the card: "I got this for you at the Harvest Festival. I know how much you love Klimt's work."

She had gotten me The Kiss? This is an apology.

Wrapped in a cocoon of assumption, I eagerly tore away at the butcher paper, my heart softening. Then I stopped abruptly. It wasn't *The Kiss*.

What the hell, I thought, taken aback by what I saw. The three-foot by five-foot framed silkscreen print was Klimt's *Judith II*, a piece that depicted an androgynous-looking femme fatale, Judith, carrying the severed head of a man, Holofernes, dangling from her hand. I admired Klimt's work, but I couldn't see beauty in this piece. It was blood-dripping gruesome. Mortified, I quickly rewrapped it, securing it tightly. I knew the story of Judith and realized that the painting in its original intent was symbolic of the historical events. But receiving it from Jocelyn, the painting's symbolism had taken on a new interpretation. I could only see the sadistic, violent end of a man by a woman. Jocelyn's mutilation and the destruction of Jack, and with it my own grief. *Amends?* Even though I knew that Jocelyn had gotten the piece weeks before our visit to the therapist's office, I felt the return of my slap.

"Diane? Still there?" Black letters shouted out another line of type.

"Yes . . . yes, I got the painting," I said, not thinking it necessary to let her know that I had given it a proper burial.

"I came to see you when I was in town a couple of months ago but I found that you had moved! Where did you go?"

"I couldn't stay there," I clicked in reply.

"I want to see you," Jocelyn's keys typed. "I'll be in San Francisco next month. Can we meet?"

Meet? The pain of betrayal resurfaced with every press of the keys at my fingertips. My heart was still raw. It's been over four years . . .

"I will have to think about it," I typed back. "I'll let you know. You said, the 16th? Is your e-mail address still the same?"

What will I be setting myself up for? I had wondered.

It had been over four years . . .

Chapter 46

Happy Trails to You

I pulled into the parking lot near the Borders bookstore at the Stonestown Galleria mall and turned off the car's ignition. I wondered, *would she be on time?* My nerves were on edge. My daughter, Kristie, recently graduated with a Bachelor of Science degree and having grown into an independent young woman, had offered to come along. Kristie did not hold back her opinion, stating more than once, "You shouldn't see her alone."

"I'll be fine," I reassured. "We're meeting in a busy bookstore."

"Still . . ." Kristie was adamant. "I don't know why you ever agreed to see her anyway. She doesn't deserve to see you ever again!"

"It's been over four years. Maybe it will resolve something for me if we talk."

"Well, if it were me," Kristie continued, "I'd want to punch her lights out."

All of my children had told me exactly what they thought, once they learned Jocelyn and I were no longer together. None had been happy about it and I knew news of this meet-up would cause their pain to resurface, too.

"I know," I said in an attempt to calm Kristie's angst. "I respect how you feel, but I need to handle this in my own way."

So here I am, I thought, *sitting alone outside of Borders bookstore, wondering what I will say.*

* * *

I ordered coffee in a porcelain cup and a pre-packaged biscotti before sitting down at a small table at the center of the cafeteria-styled room that was Borders Café. Once settled, I looked at my cell phone to see Jocelyn might have called to cancel.

"Hello, Diane!" I glanced up to see a tall woman approach the table with a latte in hand.

She looks the same, was my immediate thought. Casually dressed, Jocelyn had her hair pulled back at the neck, in a very un-Edward Scissorhands fashion. She wore pink lip gloss, and light blue-rimmed glasses framed her aquamarine eyes. *No, not the same*, I observed with interest. *She looks comfortable with herself.*

"Jocelyn," I replied, feeling tense, as she pulled a chair out and sat down.

"How are you?" she smiled.

"Good," I said. "You?"

"Glad to be here," she said, her eyes softening as her expression became serious. "Glad to see *you*," she added with an affirmative nod that punctuated her sincerity.

"What have you been up to?" I asked, not knowing what to feel or what to say, but realizing a lot can happen in four years.

"I've moved a couple of times," Jocelyn answered, as she settled back into her chair.

"You're not in Santa Clarita?" I asked.

"Santa Clarita didn't work out. Unfortunately, wanting to start a new life and not letting anyone know

250

that I had transitioned turned out to be a mistake. Eventually, as people I worked with learned I had been a man, they felt betrayed. They felt I had lied to them because I hadn't been up front. Similar to what it was like for people when I transitioned to a woman. Those that had always known me as a man felt betrayed. You would know," she said with a sad-look.

"I do know," I said, realizing the brutal irony of it. "It's as if you traded one secret life for another.

"Basically, yes," she said. "So, I retired, considering everything at the time, it seemed like the logical course of action. Then, I moved again, and started over doing things I've always wanted to do."

"Such as?" I prodded, wondering *what was it that Jocelyn had always wanted to do?*

"I read, and every day I go to the gym," she said with a smile.

A life of leisure. Her comment sent my mind back to an afternoon long before Jack had come out. We had been 'people watching' in a South City Starbucks when we noticed an older Caucasian man holding hands across a table from a much younger Asian woman. She had flowing, jet-black hair and wore a red, crocheted dress. While I had concentrated on the difference in their ages, Jack had commented, "If I were a woman, I'd find myself a rich old guy, do what I needed to do to keep him happy, and live a life of leisure." Jack used a stereotype to assume that was their story, but I was disturbed by why Jack thought it was okay for a woman to take advantage of a man in that way. *Was he serious?*

Personally, I had always thought of a relationship not *only* as two people being in love, but also as a partnership. Now I wondered, *was that another place where I had gone wrong? No,* my inner voice

251

answered. *That wasn't the person I was. It would be against my value system.*

"It sounds like you live a life of leisure." I couldn't help but say, before I asked, "Marta?"

I wondered if they were still together or, had Jocelyn found the old guy? "She has a job she loves," Jocelyn replied. "It keeps us solvent."

I took a moment to sip my coffee.

"Then it worked out for the both of you?" I finally asked.

"Yes, it has worked. We live in the same house," adding, "we're just friends."

I nodded, not knowing what this meant or what to ask next. I didn't have to.

"We're sexual outlaws, of sorts," she said, giving me her old the cat that swallowed the canary grin.

I could only guess at what she meant, but whatever it was I was certain she was proud of it. It sounded that her life was like a double-edged sword. Jocelyn had always told me she wanted a normal life, but she also reveled in the uniqueness of her situation. Jack had loved the element of surprise and the need for the attention that went with it. Something told me that *this* integral part of Jack had stayed with Jocelyn.

Jocelyn suddenly blurted out, "I'm sorry I hurt you." Her smile dropped, and her face showed remorse.

Surprised, I looked away, avoiding her eyes. *I don't want to have this conversation*, I thought. *I'm not ready to forgive her for what she did to me—to us.*

"You don't have to say anything," Jocelyn quickly added. "I don't expect you to, I just needed to say it."

Not knowing how to respond, I drank the last of my coffee, still not willing to meet her eyes and not wanting to feel the pain of her again.

Jocelyn seemed not to notice she had touched a chord in me.

"Can we . . . be friends? At least, stay in touch?" she continued.

"I don't know," I said, hesitating to give an answer. Shaken, I tried to pull myself together. *Maybe coming here today was a mistake,* I thought to myself, as I mourned within my heart, my past love for Jack, the collision of Jocelyn, and their confusing duplicity together.

"I know, it's probably a lot to ask considering everything," she said. "But I *did* care for you."

Trying to put context to her words, I acknowledged to myself that *we were never on the same page.*

"Thank you for telling me that," I said, taking a leap to change the subject. "I want to let you know that I am writing a book."

"A book?" Jocelyn looked at me, surprised.

"About our relationship, about your transition, and the actions I took to understand it."

Having begun, I took the opportunity and ran with it.

"More people are becoming aware of the term transgender, but transsexuality is still largely a mystery. You could say it's still behind closed doors. By sharing my experience, I hope I can help others who may be going through this with the person they love."

"I know it wasn't easy for you," Jocelyn started. "I'm sorry I didn't handle things better."

"It was a difficult time," I affirmed. "What I discovered is that whether someone is a wife, a lover, husband, child, mother, father, aunt, uncle, cousin, or even a friend, we significant others experience similar fears and confusion, and have common questions when someone we love decides to transition. Our world flip-flops, and our perceptions are forced to morph while we attempt to bridge a metamorphosis we may not understand. While we want to be supportive, we cannot help but question, and wonder, how will our relationships change?"

I paused, and only then dared to look her in the eye. "Would you be okay with me telling our story?"

"If you tell the truth," Jocelyn said, meeting my gaze.

"I will tell the truth," I said. "But you must understand, the story will be about my reaction to what happened. You often said everyone's reality is different. The things we went through will be from my perspective—my truth. What I felt, and how I reacted to what I didn't understand, and more than anything, what *I* did to find answers for myself. It's *my* story," I realized there were parts of my journey to understanding that Jocelyn did not know.

Jocelyn again nodded that she understood, and I stopped to take a breath.

"I want others to understand the process, and I will share the feelings and thoughts that went through my mind. I don't want anyone to have to go through what I did—the pain of the confusion, the lack of information, and mostly, the feeling they are all alone. I want people to know that they are *not* alone. I also want wives and partners to know, that if they both want it badly enough, staying with the person they love is possible. We didn't have that kind of support. I believe the key is that each must be open and honest with the other. Right from the start. Even if it hurts."

Jocelyn nodded her agreement again.

"Are you happy?" I asked suddenly.

She shrugged a yes.

"I'm glad," I said, still not convinced. "Have you realized the things you had hoped you would by your transition?"

"No, no, not everything," she admitted after pondering for a moment.

"But no regrets?" I asked.

Sadness crossed her face. "I wish you were with me."

Her comment took me by surprise.

"I can't . . ." I whispered, as emotion caught the words, and confusion spun again. I looked away.

"I know," she said, reaching for my hand. "I know, but I had to say it. I needed you to know. Can we stay in touch?" she asked again.

I nodded, pulling my hand away. I felt the need to escape.

"It was good to see you, but I must go," I said, beginning to scoot myself away from the table. Then, I stopped. "I know that it took a great deal of courage to make the life changes that you made, Jocelyn. I want you to know that I have no regrets. I am glad you are happy." I stood.

"Do you have to go so soon? I hoped we might have lunch," Jocelyn's eyes pleaded.

"I can't. I really must go," I replied. "I'll be in touch," I said, thinking, *Christmas and your birthday.*

* * *

I hurried to my car, and as the door closed behind me, I took a breath before turning the key in the ignition. I was shaking. I slipped an Andrea Bocelli CD into the player while I tried to gather and calm my thoughts.

You've held onto your sadness and anger for so long, said my inner voice. *It's been over four years! You never knew Jack. He was only a reflection of what you wanted him to be, and she is not the he you thought you knew. Isn't it time to let go of the idea of the love you thought you had?*

The year was 2004. And, as the music said, *Time to Say Goodbye.*

Chapter 47

The Cat Was Out of the Bag

As Tara had been unable to return, I sat alone at the table in *Viva*, reminiscing, until I noticed the dinner crowd begin to trickle in. Taking the hint, I gathered my purse and manuscript, took a last sip of what was left of my no-longer-cold Coke for the leftover flavored ice water, and headed for the Embarcadero BART station.

While I hadn't been able to tell Tara the whole story in one afternoon, she was the first person I had opened up to about my experience with Jack. Transsexuality was still behind closed doors and I still didn't expect that anyone was ready to hear my story. At least not yet. That Tara listened, helped. I had begun to let the cat out of the bag. Talking to her had felt good.

Riding home on BART that afternoon, I couldn't help but recall all of the good times I had with Jack, and the love I felt for him and how I had grieved at his loss. And then I marveled over Jack's transition to Jocelyn. Talking to Tara had allowed me to leave some of my pain behind. As the train rumbled its way along the track toward Daly City, I promised myself to keep putting words on paper.

It was 2006 and time to heal.

Chapter 48

Epilogue—White Bird

My nothing-to-do-with-Christmas-or-her-birthday e-mail to Jocelyn had been brief.

"Please take a look at the copy of *Conundrum* that I gave you and let me know if you see an inscription by Jan Morris. It should be on the title page."

It's 2009! It's been ten years, I thought. It makes sense I might not remember, *but how could I have forgotten something so important?* I couldn't remember the inscription Jan Morris had written for Jocelyn.

Two days later, I received a return e-mail from Jocelyn. "I don't see an inscription. Why do you ask?"

In disbelief, I wrote back, "Please check again. Perhaps it is on an inner page?"

That afternoon, another e-mail reply came from Jocelyn. "I have looked thoroughly. What is this about?"

Not quite sure how to explain what happened so many years before, I quickly typed out: "I may have the opportunity to meet Ms. Morris in the weeks ahead. I also have a copy of *Conundrum* and I was going to go ask that she autograph it. Thinking back to when I went to have yours signed, I realized I could not remember what she wrote—I was just curious."

Jocelyn's reply had sent my mind into a tailspin. I clearly recalled going to Book Passage and seeing Jan Morris that November evening in 1999. I remembered waiting in line for the opportunity to have the book signed for Jocelyn. I remembered how stressed I had been. But that is where my mind drew a blank. The book was not signed? *Of course, it was*, I thought. *There must be some mistake.*

But before Jocelyn could respond, I sent an additional request. "If there is no inscription, and if you would be willing to send me your copy of *Conundrum*, I will take your book to have it signed also."

A part of me was in disbelief and thought Jocelyn had not looked thoroughly for the signature.

Two days later a small package to me from Jocelyn arrived at my doorstep. As I once again held the hard cover first edition, I examined it closely. It had been printed in the United States. It resembled my copy only in its text. Printed in New York, the book's dust cover was black with the title in a colorful font. My own copy of *Conundrum* had been unearthed several months after I found Jocelyn's, when a bookstore owner on Eddy Street, who had taken my name and number, came across a copy and gave me a call. My volume was also a first edition printing, but by Faber & Faber in London. Its dust jacket was white.

Opening Jocelyn's book, I discovered she was correct. There was no autograph. As I searched through the pages of the book, I slowly began to recall why I had forgotten. Shortly before that Christmas holiday, we had one of our then, all-too-frequent arguments. Jocelyn had left town in a huff to stay with friends. I had not been with her when she opened my gift and had not watched her gush in surprise at finding the long-sought treasure. Nor had I witnessed Jocelyn's delight upon discovering Ms. Morris had personalized it. What I did remember was how unhappy that holiday had been and why I had chosen to forget it.

My own copy of *Conundrum*, after reading it cover-to-cover, had sat quietly on the bookshelf for these many years since. Now I was, once again hoping to meet Ms. Jan Morris, who was in town to promote her newest book, *Coast to Coast*. I arrived at Book Passage in time to see the tall white-haired woman enter the bookstore. I held the two books, which I had wrapped tight in a small brown paper bag, close to my heart. I walked towards the back of the store to the event room where rows of neatly placed chairs, many with placards that said, "Reserved," filled the room.

I had arrived early as I wanted to sit close, but even so, I had to sit six rows back. I watched as the room filled to its capacity. My heart was pounding.

It's been ten years, I thought, as I watched Ms. Morris take her place on stage. Don George, editor and author of *Lonely Planet's Guide to Travel Writing*, introduced her. I was struck by the appearance of Jan Morris; not as small in stature as I had remembered, she looked as if she may have just stepped off a cross-country plane flight and was dressed casually. She wore a T-shirt she later revealed was given to her by her daughter. It read, "This is a No-Hug Zone." I smiled as I remembered that when Jack transitioned, so did behaviors. Jocelyn would hug almost everyone when she left his or her presence. It was as if she believed that it's something women do.

It felt like déjà vu. The crowd asked questions about her new book, and Jan Morris graciously answered with humor. As before, *Conundrum*, was never mentioned. Then, suddenly, one man called out, "When did you first begin to feel you were a woman?

261

Was it after your surgery, or when you first were with a man?"

The crowd gasped at his rudeness, and the room became silent and tense. Avoiding a confrontation, Ms. Morris, reined herself in, and with a stony look, but a voice laced with grace, replied, "I have addressed my journey to womanhood in my book *Conundrum*. You will have to read the book to find out."

Good for you! I thought. *Well put!* I was pleased she had been able so easily to handle the bully.

Someone else in the audience asked where one might find a copy of *Conundrum*. "Isn't it out of print?" was the question. When it was suggested one might check used bookstores, I smiled, knowing I held two copies on my lap.

As the moderator concluded the interview, I rose with the crowd forming a line, and waited my turn. Approaching Jan Morris, I smiled. I was no longer nervous or uncertain, I showed her my two copies of *Conundrum*, and explained why I had come. Ms. Morris, pen poised, was quietly attentive as I shared how I had come to see her in November 1999 hoping to have Jocelyn's copy signed as a special gift for that upcoming Christmas holiday.

"I don't know why I left before having you sign the book," I admitted. "Other than fear. At the time, I did not know how to express why I was there. My heart and psyche were in turmoil, as I struggled to keep our relationship. I had no information or tools to work with, and no support." Then, I told Jan Morris I was writing the story of my experience around Jocelyn's transition.

"How many chapters have you written?" Ms. Morris asked.

"Over twenty," I responded.

"Are they long or short?" she asked with a smile.

"A bit of both," I said.

Her smile broadened. My heart beat fast. I was grateful for her warm smile, and her interest. It was if I had received her benediction for all that I had been through, and affirmation for writing about the experience.

"Do you have a preference as to how I sign this book?" she asked, as I handed her Jocelyn's copy.

"She asked me to ask you if you had any words of wisdom for her."

Jan Morris took a moment, looking solemn, and then, wrote. She closed the book before handing it back to me. Then, she took my copy of *Conundrum* and opened it to its title page.

"Do you have a request for how I sign your copy?" she asked. There was that smile again.

"Ms. Morris, your book was part of the puzzle that was Jack. It could have been the key that might have unlocked the conversation about Jack's secret desire to be female years before he was able to actually express it to me. If only we had located your book sooner. Now I'm just happy to have found these copies, happy to be here, and very happy to finally meet you. Please, write whatever you think would be appropriate."

She nodded, smiled, and then wrote, "Diane! The missing piece, Jan Morris, 2009."

I thanked her again and walked away quickly, as I felt tears of gratitude for a circle closing overwhelm me. I had finally achieved what I had set out to do so many years before. Stopping among the stacks at Book Passage, I took a moment to stop and open Jack's copy of *Conundrum* and read Jan Morris' message.

Perfectly said, I thought. Ms. Morris' message to Jocelyn was one that echoed in my own heart: "Enjoy Life!"

263

Letter to Readers

I hope that those of you who have taken the time to read my story, find it does more than satisfy your curiosity. If you are a significant other, you are unwittingly in a transition of your own. You deserve support too. I hope my story will leave you with some questions answered.

I would appreciate knowing if my story touches you, or how it helped you. You can leave your comments at **dianakellyauthor.com**. If you feel my book might benefit others, I would appreciate you leaving your review of my story where you purchased my book. My book is also available in e-book formats.

Thank you,

Diane

Acknowledgements

First, I thank my children for their unconditional love and support through the years and for their words, "You need to write the story, Mom. It is a story that needs to be shared." I know each of them thought I would never get it finished. I want to thank each for their individual contributions, whether it be by proofreading, initial editing, book cover design, or just sitting down with me to reminisce about the past situations they remembered. I couldn't have done it without you.

My thanks to Eric Baxter, a Poetry Farm founder, Novato, California, for his encouragement to attend an open mic at Dr. Insomniac's Fine Coffee Tea, Smoothies Cafe in 2007. It was a public 'coming out' which convinced me there was an audience for the book and that many people want to understand, be supportive, and would be accepting. Thank you, Farmers, for listening and wanting to hear more. Thank you, Cassandra Cushing, better known as Cassie, owner of Kaleidoscope Coffee, Point Richmond, California, for providing yet another open mic venue that promotes creativity through readings and music on a weekly stage and, so importantly, supports an environment of diversity.

Thank you, Susan Bishop Sherman, for your compassion and the thoughts you shared with me that afternoon in 1998, after I told you that Jack had just come out to me about his secret desire. I'll never forget the look on your face, and you nailed it by your comment when you said, "For you, it must be as if suddenly the sky has turned green and the grass has turned blue."

A special thanks to Sarah Hill-Lambert, for your willingness to listen to my story early on when I thought no one would, and your continual encouragement to get it written and published. A shout out to Ray Slater, author of *Via Dolorosa*, and *Redemption Rock: A Novel of 17th Century New England*, and John Sakellar, author of *The Empty Quarter*, for your friendship and support, for staying true to our book group for a year, and being bi-weekly sounding boards and giving your unbiased critiques. I can't thank you enough. To Anita Erola, poet and friend, thank you for your encouragement, and listening ear as over the years, I have verbally worked through the rewrite of chapters with you over coffee. To Lynne Ashdown, friend, and author of *One American Woman Fifty Italian Men: A Journey of Cycling, Love and Will*, thank you for your interest and your critical eye. To J.W., thank you for your spot-on comments of my very first sixty pages of written draft which provided valuable direction. To my friends in the Kink Community of San Francisco, thank you. I will always be grateful for your insight and acceptance in my exploration into a world so many wonder about, but never experience. Also, my appreciation goes out to the members of the LGBTQI community of Richmond, CA for your acceptance and support for my open mic readings of my story to the local community. It has been humbling. Monica P., thank you for sharing your insights of the LGBTQI community. Additionally, I want to thank two remarkable women, Ellen Shaver and Kim McBride, for sharing with me parts of your own journey, my deepest gratitude. I applaud your courage and wish for you the best that life can offer.

Thank you to my wonderful editors, Suzanne Logan, Lily O'Brien, and Ray Slater for helping me hone the final product. To my son, Donald, for his technical advice, cover design work, and help along the way in the self-publishing process—my heart-felt appreciation. I couldn't have finished this without any of you.

Last, but foremost, to 'J'—Thank you for the chance to love you, and for the unanticipated adventure that knowing you brought into my life. You found your authentic self. I found understanding, and that I had a story to tell that I hope will benefit others. My best wishes to you for a wonderful life.

Diane

Notes

I have chosen to notate books and music as referenced in my story. Each book, and in particular, each piece of music listed, is a story unto itself and conveys some of the mood and feelings I experienced.

Books Referenced

Joyce, James. *Ulysses*. First Vintage International Edition, June 1990. Random House, Inc., NY, New York. (Trieste—Zurich—Paris, 1914-1921) pp. 782-783. (Page 6)

Mappelthorpe, Robert. *Some Women*. Bulfinch Press. Little, Brown & Company, Boston, Toronto, London. 1989. (Page 179)

Morris, Jan. *Conundrum*. Faber and Faber Ltd, 1974. Butler & Tanner Ltd, England, p.13. (Page 179)

Music Referenced

The Best of The Three Tenors. *O Sole Mio*. (Carreras – Domingo – Pavarotti) - Decca Music Group Limited, 2002. (Page 9)

Mayfield, Percy. *Please Send Me Someone to Love*. Performed by Sade in the movie *Philadelphia*. 1993 Sony Music Entertainment. (Page 38)

Depeche Mode. *Walking in My Shoes*. (Martin Gore) From album 'Songs of Faith and Devotion', 1993. (Page 108)

Charles, Ray. *Drown in My Own Tears*. (Henry Glover) Fort Knox Music, Inc/Trio Music Company, Inc-BMI Atlantic 1085, Released 1986. (Page 225)

Williams, Andy. Rendition of *Moon River*. Henry Mancini/Johnny Mercer, RCA Victor Records, 1961. (Page 170)

The Kazu Matsui Project. *Tribal Mozart*. Unity Entertainment Corporation. 1997 Countdown Records. (Page 190)

Bocelli, Andrea and Sarah Brightman. *Time to Say Goodbye*. From 'Romanza', Track 15. 1996 Insieme Srl. (Page 235)

Mae, Vanessa. *White Bird*. By David La Flamme and Linda La Flamme. Parlophone Records, Ltd., Warner Music Group, 2001. (Page 236)

Special Mention

Christian Haren (February 1, 1935 – February 27, 1996) was an American actor, model and community activist. Among many of his notable accomplishments in life, one being the model in Marlboro cigarette ads and known as The Marlboro Man, Mr. Haren became an activist for AIDS prevention after being diagnosed with AIDS. He started "The Wedge" a "safe sex" AIDS prevention organization for teens in San Francisco. *RIP*.

Dictionary of Terms

Androgynous—Having a combination of masculine and feminine characteristics. Usually used to describe characters or persons who have no specific gender.

BDSM—Stands for bondage, discipline or domination, sadism and masochism.

Bi-capable—A word I coined to describe a heterosexual significant other who chooses to stay in an intimate physical relationship with a previously heterosexual male partner after his M2F surgery, even though the heterosexual significant other does not and would not define herself in any other circumstance as 'bi" sexual, or lesbian.

Cisgender—A person who expresses gender identity that matches biological sex. Female identifies as a woman. Male identifies as a man.

Cross-dresser—A person who wears the clothing of the opposite sex, but does not imply one's gender identity.

Eulenspiegel Society (TES)—The longest-running BDSM education and support group in the United States. Founded in 1971, it is based in New York City.

Fetish—An object or bodily part, where the real or fantasied presence is psychologically necessary for sexual gratification, and that is also an object of fixation to the extent that it may interfere with complete sexual expression.

Gay—A homosexual person, or one who directs sexual desire towards another person of the same sex.

Gender—The behavioral, cultural and psychological characteristics that pertain to or differentiate the state of being male, female, or intersex.

Gender bender—A person who behaves as someone from the opposite sex, bending expected gender roles.

Gender dysphoria—Gender identity disorder; distress when assigned sex and gender do not match the person's gender identity.

Homosexual—Relates to a tendency to direct sexual desire towards another of the same sex.

Kink—Term for non-normative sexual behavior, often in association with BDSM or an activity or interest within BDSM

Lesbian—A female homosexual; relating to homosexuality between females.

Metamorphosis—A change of physical form, structure or substance; a striking alteration in appearance, character or circumstances.

Pansexuality—Exhibiting or implying many forms of sexual expression.

Polyamory—The practice of having more than one non-monogamous, multi-partner or non-exclusive sexual/or romantic relationship at a time.

The Community—In this story it refers to the S&M community.

Sex—Either of the two major forms of individuals that are distinguished respectively as female or male within the human species.

Significant Other—Used as a gender-neutral term for a person's partner in an intimate relationship without disclosing or presuming anything.

Submissive—Inclined or ready to submit or yield to the authority of another; unresistingly or humbly obedient

S&M—This term stands for "sadomasochism" which is the derivation of pleasure from the infliction of physical or mental pain, either on others or on oneself.

Transsexual—A person with a psychological need to belong to the opposite sex, who may feel the need to undergo sex reassignment surgery in order to modify the sex organs, in order to align their body with their identified sex or gender.

Transvestite—A person who adopts the dress and often the behavior, which is typical of the opposite sex for purposes or emotional or sexual gratification.

About the Author

Diana Kelly lives in the Bay Area of San Francisco, California. Never considering herself a writer, she found she had personal stories to tell about particular life experiences. In *The Sky Turned Green & The Grass Turned Blue: Diane's Story*, she shares her personal journey to understanding when faced with her lover's transition as a male to female transsexual. Wanting to inform and educate others, Diana shares her experiences about subjects that are still behind closed doors, and answers the questions that few dare to ask.

www.ingramcontent.com/pod-product-compliance
Lightning Source LLC
Chambersburg PA
CBHW030239030426
42336CB00009B/166